entertaining

acknowledgments

With thanks to Matt Handbury and Jackie Frank, for such a brilliant opportunity; to Jane Roarty, for her inspiration and most passionate support; to Sara Beaney, a brilliant designer, for making my book beautiful; to Michèle, for all the weekends and late nights of toil; to Rowena, my editor, who kept me motivated; to Catie, Anne, Anna, Mark and all of the rest of the Murdoch Books team, for your patience and for such a great opportunity; to Mum and Dad, for the endless stream of support and understanding – I guess I'll always be a running-late sort of person – thanks for waiting; to my friends William and Sibella, who tasted and tested, and supported me through the book; to my partner and friend Billy – words can't describe – thanks; to Jody, my inspiration, colleague, friend, and strength, who enabled me to get this far – thank you; to the Antico family, for searching the markets for the most amazing fresh fruit and vegetables, and for entertaining me when I come to the shop; to Con and James of Demcos Seafood Providores, for the freshest, sweetest seafood; to Petrina, who stuck with the cracking pace, for the long and sometimes painful task of photography, thank you for your input and energy in making this book a visual feast.

Recipes and Styling: Donna Hay
Photographer: Petrina Tinslay
Designer: Michèle Chan
Editor: Rowena Lennox

HarperCollins books may be purchased for educational, business, or sales promotional use. For information please write: Special Markets Department, HarperCollins Publishers Inc., 10 East 53rd Street, New York, NY 10022.

Originally published in Australia in 1998 by Murdoch Books® , a division of Murdoch Magazines Pty Ltd.

FIRST U.S. EDITION PUBLISHED 2003

Library of Congress Cataloging-in-Publication Data has been applied for

ISBN 0-06-056630-2

03 04 05 06 07/10 9 8 7 6 5 4 3 2 1

entertaining

donna hay

WILLIAM MORROW
An Imprint of HarperCollins*Publishers*

contents

introduction

Entertaining is about sharing food, wine, good conversation and a laugh or two with friends. Great memories are often made around a table of delicious food and drinks.

The recipes in this book range from simple yet stylish weeknight dinner solutions, to food for the most formal dining experience. You'll find information about planning menus and selecting wines, as well as all the basics you'll need for any culinary occasion. *Entertaining* offers inspirational recipes with innovative serving ideas and refreshing liquid suggestions. There are menu ideas for each chapter, but please feel free to create your own menus from any of the chapters.

More information about ingredients and cooking terms marked with an asterisk* can be found in the glossary. Turn to the glossary for basic recipes, which are also marked in the text with an asterisk*.

menus

Putting together a menu is easy. If you follow a few simple guides, you can choose foods that will complement each other and flow to form a complete dining experience.
Avoid doubling up on flavours, cream-based recipes and ingredients. For example, if you are serving a Thai chicken salad as a starter, don't serve a spice-crusted grilled chicken breast as a main meal. Also, avoid doubling up on some cooking methods such as deep-frying. It is fine to have one deep-fried course but serving two courses of deep-fried food would be too heavy.

planning a menu

Continuity is important in a menu. If you were to serve an Asian meal flavoured with chillies, lime and fresh Asian herbs, a chocolate dessert would not be in continuity with the menu. You could try, for example, a lime and green apple sorbet or grilled mangoes instead.

As a guide, serve lighter foods first. By lighter foods, I don't mean not well-flavoured foods, but foods that are not too heavy and complex. A very complex and lavish starter followed by a similar style of main meal may be a little heavy on the stomach. It's better to serve a simply flavoured starter followed by a more complex main meal. The flavours need to build on each other and develop through the menu. If you are aware that the people you are dining with enjoy very rich foods, you could always bend this guideline.

The food you choose and the style in which you decide to present it should be in keeping with the style of dining you wish to have. For example, an Asian banquet of delicately steamed morsels to be shared usually results in a less formal occasion than a three or four course meal. To make an occasion more informal, have a table where food is set out for the guests to help themselves. Alternatively, have large platters and bowls at the table where you are sitting, so people can pick and choose what and how much they would like to eat.

serving success

A few little serving tips can help ensure the success of your dining experience.

To keep hot foods hot, warm the plates. If you are serving ice cream or sorbet in summer, you could chill the bowls or plates before serving.

Remember to change wine glasses when you serve a different wine. The residues of the previous wine could ruin the flavour of the new one.

If the occasion is formal and you have definite ideas on where you would like people to sit, place name cards on the table instead of ushering people around the table.

Serve drinks and something for your guests to nibble with their drinks as soon as they arrive. This will help them relax and feel comfortable.

Whatever drinks you are serving, place water glasses and water on the table.

If you are serving seafood with shells, have bowls on the table for discarding the unwanted bits and have finger bowls and warm towels so your guests can clean their hands.

timing is everything

Shop for dry goods and foods that will keep at least the day before your planned event. Pick up vegetables, meat and seafood on the day.

When planning your menu, choose some dishes that you can make ahead of time. Making the dessert or part of the starter or main meal beforehand will help the meal go smoothly and will ensure that you have time to enjoy yourself.

Remember to place wine, water and other drinks in the refrigerator or on ice well ahead of time.

Set the table with cutlery, napkins, underplates, glasses, serving ware, salt and pepper, condiments and anything else it requires before your guests arrive. With cutlery, start with the first course on the outside and work your way in. Bread plates should be on the left side of the setting, and wine glasses on the top right.

Remember to allow time to shower and dress before your guests are at the door.

wines

food and wine

When choosing wine to accompany your food, be aware that many different flavour levels are described by a simple word such as salad. A salad might be delicately flavoured greens and chervil with a light dressing and a soft quail egg, or it might be a robust combination of roast fennel slices, soft oven-roasted tomatoes, marinated olives and pan-fried haloumi cheese with a rich balsamic dressing. The wines you would select for these salads would be quite different. Use the following general recommendations as a guide only. Map out your food and wine choices together. Serve the wine before the food so your guests can taste it before adding the flavours of the food to their palates. There are no hard and fast rules about choosing wine. Try out some different combinations and remember, just because you had one bottle of sauvignon blanc that didn't excite the senses, the other 20 bottles of sauvignon blanc at the wine merchant's aren't all going to taste the same. Choosing wine is a personal thing—be adventurous!

whites

SEMILLON

Varies in colour according to the time the grape was picked and the age of the wine. Semillon ends up in bottles as two different wines. Ripe-picked grapes, with grassy, citrus flavours, make a young wine that fills the mouth with fresh flavours, usually ready to drink a year or two after harvest. Young semillon is also blended with sauvignon blanc and chardonnay. Early-picked semillon grapes, a little on the green side, start with a fairly bland taste but, with a good age, the wine takes on a honey and vanilla nose and has a rich and nutty flavour. General recommendations: fish, poultry, pork, rabbit, vegetables and salads.

SAUVIGNON BLANC

A crisp, dry wine, pale straw in colour, that has a variety of flavours from fresh-cut grass to asparagus and tropical fruits. A good sauvignon blanc should be fresh and almost cool tasting with lively flavours that awaken the mouth. General recommendations: salads, vegetables, Asian foods (for example, Thai, Vietnamese, Chinese and Malaysian) and smoked salmon.

CHARDONNAY

A broad, full-bodied wine, which has a range of melon and peach flavours when young, and buttery, fig and honey flavours with a bit of age. Chardonnay is often aged in wood or oak. This has sometimes been overdone, giving rise to the unwooded chardonnay, which has less obvious flavours. General recommendations: salads, vegetables, white meats and full-flavoured seafood.

RIESLING

A crisp and clean wine with a lemon and lime acidic taste that leaves the mouth fresh with a well-balanced fruitiness. This dry wine has a greenish tinge when young, and a floral and citrus aroma. If the grapes are cut late from the vine or infected with the botrytis strain, riesling makes a wonderful sweet dessert wine. General recommendations: seafood, Thai and Chinese foods, spicy foods and salads.

CHENIN BLANC

With a light citrus taste, this simple wine exhibits a dry palate, which is soft and full. Chenin blanc is a drink-now style of wine, perfect with a simple seafood meal. General recommendations: all seafood and mildly spiced foods.

VERDELHO

This wine has a very sleek texture. Flowery, citrus and fruit tastes make a dry wine with good body. General recommendations: pasta dishes, cream sauces, fish and fried foods.

SPARKLING

A great way to start a meal, bubbly white refreshes the mouth and plays on the tongue. Most sparkling wines are ready to drink when they are released, although some vintage wines need to be cellared so their tastes develop. General recommendations: pre-dinner morsels, seafood and celebrations.

glasses

Drink wine from glasses that are made for drinking wine. It really will make a difference when you are drinking quality wine. Be sure that the glasses you choose slope inwards towards the top rim so all the wonderful aromas of the wine head in the direction of your nose.

tasting wine

To start, pour a small amount of wine into a glass. Look at the colour of the wine as it will often tell you a lot, for example, a green tint to a sauvignon blanc will indicate a fresh and perhaps grassy taste. If it is in good condition, the wine should be crystal clear and bright.

Next, swirl the wine around the glass, hold it up to your nose and have a good sniff—just like testing a fine perfume. Learn to recognise the aromas of different wine, for example, a lemony, grassy young sauvignon blanc contrasted with the peppery, berry and wooded aromas of a good shiraz.

Now, take a very small sip of the wine and allow it to move around your mouth, making sure it covers all the tastebuds on your tongue. While the wine is in your mouth, take a short, small in-breath and allow the aromas of the wine to fill your mouth all the way to the back of your throat. You will not only be tasting the wine's characteristics but you will also feel its texture, for example, the viscosity and thick smoothness of a sticky dessert wine or the velvety softness of a pinot noir.

After all this hard work and assessment, swallow.

reds

PINOT NOIR

A smooth, light red wine that has a range of flavours, from berry fruits and cherry to spice and earthiness. Pinot noir is a wine with intense flavour and a clean, fresh and velvety soft mouth feel. General recommendations: full-flavoured fish such as tuna and Atlantic salmon, duck and game meats, some spicy foods, pâté, terrines and pasta dishes.

CABERNET SAUVIGNON

With blackcurrant and faint new-oak or cedarwood smells, cabernet sauvignon is a great robust and flexible wine with medium-to-full body, a lingering full finish, and loads of tannin and acidity. General recommendations: beef, lamb and some game meats.

MERLOT

Merlot is most commonly found blended with cabernet sauvignon. It is a soft low-acid and low-tannin wine but still has a full, rich, round flavour. When it isn't blended, merlot is extremely round and mellow. General recommendations: red meats, Italian food and cheeses.

SHIRAZ

A dark and full-flavoured wine, exhibiting berry and spice flavours that are sometimes even peppery and earthy, with a soft oak finish. Shiraz has a generous flavour with softer tannin and acid than cabernet sauvignon, making these two perfect blending partners. General recommendations: beef, veal, game meats, mature cheeses and smoked foods.

GRENACHE

A wine that is often blended with a shiraz or mourvèdre (mataro) because of its full-spice and ripe-fruit flavours. Once blended, grenache improves to become a rich, spicy wine. General recommendations: Middle Eastern food, garlic-rich foods and spiced meats.

coffee & cake

1

basics

Coffee is the seed from a type of evergreen cherry tree that grows in a narrow subtropical belt around the world. At first, small clusters of jasmine-like flowers appear on the tree, then small green cherries. The cherries take six to nine months to ripen, changing from green to yellow to red until they become dark and almost black. The coffee cherries are picked by hand as they ripen at different times. Each coffee cherry contains two green coffee beans and it takes 4000 coffee beans to produce 500g (1 lb) of roasted coffee.

processing

After they are picked, the coffee cherries are processed to remove the cherry flesh so that only the beans remain. This is done either by drying the cherries and removing the fruit by husking, or by soaking them. The green beans are then sorted and graded by hand and transported all around the world for roasting.

roasting

Roasting caramelises the sugars and carbohydrates in the coffee bean, creating coffee oil, which is where coffee's flavour and aroma come from. A lightly roasted bean, the colour of cinnamon to light chocolate, is used for espresso, as lighter roasts produce a sharper and more acidic taste than darker roasts. The darker the roast, the less caffeine and acidity.

blending

Coffee beans differ in flavour according to the coffee tree's growing conditions and location. A full-flavoured and balanced coffee is produced by blending. Beans of the same type grown in different places are often blended for the perfect coffee. Many espresso coffees contain three to seven different beans to create the necessary complexity.

grind guide

Percolator: coarse
Electric drip or French press (plunger): medium
Espresso and filter-cone drip: very fine

10 steps to better coffee

- Use fresh coffee beans. Store beans at a cool room temperature away from strong food odours. Unless you need to store beans for a prolonged period of time, they should not be frozen, as freezing affects the taste of the coffee.
- Air and moisture are the enemies of coffee, so keep it in a well-sealed container.
- Coffee is at its best when consumed within 24 to 72 hours after roasting. The flavour diminishes substantially after seven to 10 days. Old coffee beans look oily.
- Be sure your coffee is ground to fit your purpose and taste.
- For a great coffee, grind your beans just before making it.
- Purchase quality coffee to guarantee a good result.
- Use the right amount of coffee—a good general guide is 2 level tablespoons of coffee per cup.
- Be sure that your coffee-making equipment (plungers, espresso machines and so on) is clean and free from any ground coffee or coffee oils.
- Warm your cup with boiling water before pouring coffee.
- Before serving, give the cup of coffee a stir to ensure that you distribute the heavier coffee oils, and therefore stronger flavours, throughout the cup.

percolator

coffee beans

French press (plunger)

espresso machine

ground coffee

coconut and golden syrup wafers

chocolate shortbread sandwiches

coconut and golden syrup wafers

125g (4 oz) butter, chopped
1 cup caster (superfine) sugar
1/2 cup (4 fl oz) golden syrup
1 1/3 cups plain (all-purpose) flour
1 cup desiccated coconut
2 egg whites

Preheat the oven to 180°C (350°F). Place the butter and sugar in the bowl of an electric mixer and beat until creamy. Add the golden syrup and beat until combined. Stir the flour, coconut and egg whites into the mixture and refrigerate for 10 minutes.
Place tablespoons of the mixture onto trays lined with non-stick baking paper and spread with a palette knife into rough 5cm (2 in) circles. (The wafers will spread, so leave space between them.) Bake for 8–10 minutes or until a light golden colour. Cool the wafers on a wire rack. Serve with a macchiato. Makes 30.

chocolate shortbread sandwiches

125g (4 oz) butter
2/3 cup icing (confectioner's) sugar
3/4 cup plain (all-purpose) flour
1/4 cup rice flour
1/3 cup cocoa powder
filling
125g (4 oz) dark chocolate
1/4 cup (2 fl oz) cream (single or pouring)

Preheat the oven to 160°C (315°F). Place the butter and icing sugar in the bowl of an electric mixer and beat until light and creamy. Add the flour, rice flour and cocoa powder and mix until a smooth dough forms.
Roll out the dough between sheets of non-stick baking paper until 2mm (1/8 in) thick. Cut the dough into 6cm (2 1/2 in) circles and place on a baking tray lined with non-stick baking paper. Bake for 15 minutes or until the biscuits are firm to the touch. Cool on wire racks.
To make the filling, place the chocolate and cream in a saucepan over low heat and stir until smooth. Refrigerate until firm.
To serve, sandwich 2 biscuits together with a spoonful of chocolate filling. Makes 12.

parchment blueberry and passionfruit muffins

parchment paper and string
1 3/4 cups plain (all-purpose) flour, sifted
1 1/2 teaspoons baking powder
1 cup caster (superfine) sugar
1 teaspoon ground cinnamon
1 cup sour cream
60g (2 oz) soft butter
2 teaspoons grated lemon rind
1 egg
1/3 cup (2 3/4 fl oz) passionfruit pulp
1 cup blueberries

Preheat the oven to 180°C (350°F). Roll small lengths of parchment paper into 8 cylinders measuring 8cm (3 in) high and 6cm (2 1/2 in) wide. Secure with string. Place the parchment cylinders in 1/2-cup capacity ramekins to fit on a lined baking tray.
Place the flour, baking powder, sugar and cinnamon in a bowl and mix to combine. Place the sour cream, butter, lemon rind, egg and passionfruit in a separate bowl and mix to combine.
Add the sour cream mixture to the dry ingredients and mix until just combined. Sprinkle the blueberries over the mixture and spoon into the parchment cylinders until just over three-quarters full. Bake for 35–40 minutes or until the muffins are cooked when tested with a skewer. Serve warm with caffè lattes for breakfast or morning snacks. Makes 8.

espresso granita

3 cups (24 fl oz) hot water
1 cup sugar
2 cups (16 fl oz) prepared strong coffee

Place the water, sugar and coffee in a saucepan over low heat and stir until the sugar is dissolved. Bring to the boil and allow to simmer for 3 minutes.
Pour the mixture into a metal container and freeze for 3 hours. Mash with a fork and return to the freezer for another 3 hours. Serve with a summer breakfast or as a pick-me-up on a hot afternoon. Serves 6.

parchment blueberry and passionfruit muffins

espresso syrup cakes

155g (5 oz) butter
2/3 cup caster (superfine) sugar
1 teaspoon vanilla essence
1 egg
1½ cups plain (all-purpose) flour, sifted
1½ teaspoons baking powder
2 tablespoons prepared espresso
2 tablespoons milk
espresso syrup
1 cup (8 fl oz) prepared strong espresso
⅓ cup sugar
1–2 tablespoons coffee liqueur

Preheat the oven to 180°C (350°F). Place the butter and sugar in a bowl and beat until light and creamy. Add the vanilla and egg and beat well. Fold the flour and baking powder into the butter mixture with the espresso and milk. Spoon the mixture into eight x 8cm (3 in) round cake tins or ½-cup capacity muffin pans and bake for 20 minutes or until the cakes are cooked when tested with a skewer. To make the syrup, place the espresso, sugar and liqueur in a saucepan over low heat and stir until the sugar is dissolved. Allow the syrup to simmer for 4–6 minutes or until thickened. To serve, invert the warm cakes onto serving plates and top with the espresso syrup and thick (double) cream. Makes 12.

espresso shots

4 tablespoons coffee beans
¾ cup (6 fl oz) cream (single or pouring
70g (2¼ oz) dark chocolate
3 tablespoons coffee or chocolate liqueur

Place the coffee beans and cream in a saucepan over low heat and simmer for 4–5 minutes. Allow to stand for 20 minutes. Strain.
Return the cream to the pan, add the chocolate and stir until smooth. Stir the liqueur through the cream. Pour the mixture into 6 shot glasses and refrigerate until set. Serve as a summer-afternoon cooler or as an after-dinner shot. Serves 6.

Portuguese custard tarts

1 quantity (350g or 12 oz) sweet flaky pastry* or
    ready-prepared puff pastry
filling
⅓ cup sugar
⅓ cup (2¾ fl oz) water
2 cups (16 fl oz) milk
2 tablespoons cornflour (cornstarch)
2 egg yolks
1 teaspoon vanilla essence

Roll out the pastry on a lightly floured surface until 3mm (⅛ in) thick. Cut into 10cm (4 in) circles and place in patty tins so the pastry comes up the side of the tin.
To make the filling, place the sugar and water in a saucepan over low heat and stir until the sugar is dissolved. Simmer the syrup for 1 minute. Mix a little of the milk with the cornflour to make a smooth paste. Whisk together the remaining milk, the cornflour paste, sugar syrup, egg yolks and vanilla. Place in a saucepan over low heat and stir until the mixture thickens. Cover the surface of the custard with plastic wrap and allow to cool.
Preheat the oven to 200°C (400°F). Spoon the filling into the pastry shells. Bake for 20 minutes or until the custard is golden and firm. Makes 8.

frozen caffè latte

2 cups (16 fl oz) milk
⅓ cup (2¾ fl oz) prepared strong espresso, chilled
6 ice cubes

Place the milk in the freezer for 3 hours or until frozen. Place the frozen milk, coffee and ice in a blender and blend until smooth. Pour into 2 chilled glasses and serve immediately. Serves 2.

après café

6 tablespoons coarse-ground coffee
1 cinnamon stick
100g (3½ oz) dark chocolate
4½ cups (36 fl oz) milk

Place the coffee, cinnamon, chocolate and milk in a saucepan and stir over medium heat until the milk starts to boil. Pour the mixture through a fine strainer and serve in 4 warmed cups or glasses. Serve on a cold afternoon. Serves 4.

portuguese custard tart

brioche with chocolate centres

espresso granita

espresso shots

frozen caffè latte

après café

little nectarine cake

little nectarine cakes

125g (4 oz) butter, chopped
1 cup sugar
1 teaspoon vanilla essence
2 eggs
1⅓ cups plain (all-purpose) flour
1½ teaspoons baking powder
1 cup sour cream
⅓ cup almond meal
3–4 nectarines, sliced
1 tablespoon demerara sugar*

Preheat the oven to 180°C (350°F). Place the butter, sugar and vanilla in the bowl of an electric mixer and beat until light and creamy. Add the eggs, one at a time, and beat well. Sift the flour and baking powder over the butter mixture and fold through with the sour cream and almonds. Line 8 x 8.5cm (3 in) round cake or muffin tins with non-stick baking paper. Divide the mixture between the tins. Top with the nectarine slices and sprinkle with the demerara sugar. Bake for 20–25 minutes or until cooked when tested with a skewer. Remove the cakes from the tins and serve warm with coffee. Makes 8.

brioche with chocolate centres

2 cups plain (all-purpose) flour
1½ teaspoons active dry yeast
½ cup (4 fl oz) warm milk
1 teaspoon vanilla essence
3 tablespoons sugar
2 egg yolks
125g (4 oz) butter, chopped and softened
8 large chunks of dark chocolate about 15g (½ oz) each

Place the flour and yeast in the bowl of an electric mixer fitted with a dough hook. Place the milk, vanilla and sugar in a separate bowl and mix until combined. Add the milk mixture and egg yolks to the flour mixture and beat on medium speed until the dough is a smooth ball. Continue beating, adding the butter, a little at a time, until incorporated and well beaten. Alternatively, mix the flour mixture and the milk mixture in a bowl until a soft dough forms. Transfer the dough to a lightly floured surface and knead until smooth. Add the butter, a few pieces at a time, and knead until combined. Cover the dough and set aside for 1½–2 hours or until doubled in size.
Preheat the oven to 180°C (350°F). Knead the dough on a lightly floured surface until soft and elastic. Divide into 8 pieces and flatten slightly in the palm of your hand. Place a piece of chocolate in the middle of each piece of dough and fold over the excess dough to enclose.
Place the brioche in 8 greased and floured dariole moulds* or brioche tins. Cover and set aside for 1 hour or until well risen.
Bake for 15–20 minutes or until the brioche are golden brown. Serve warm with strong caffè lattes. Makes 8.

chocolate and peach panforte

rice paper*
1 cup (8 fl oz) liquid glucose
3/4 cup sugar
2 cups blanched almonds, toasted and roughly chopped
1 1/2 cups chopped dried peaches
1 1/2 cups plain (all-purpose) flour, sifted
1/3 cup cocoa powder
1 teaspoon ground cinnamon
180g (6 oz) dark chocolate, melted

Preheat the oven to 180°C (350°F). Line the base and sides of an 18cm x 28cm (7 in x 11 in) slice tin with rice paper and set aside.
Place the glucose and sugar in a saucepan and stir over low heat until the sugar is dissolved. Bring the syrup to the boil and simmer for 2 minutes or until thickened slightly.
Place the almonds, peaches, flour, cocoa and cinnamon in a bowl. Add the syrup and chocolate and mix until combined. Firmly press the mixture into the prepared tin and bake for 20 minutes or until the panforte is spongy to the touch. Allow to cool in the tin. Cut and serve with coffee. Makes 20 squares.

caramel melting moments

250g (8 oz) butter
2/3 cup brown sugar
2 cups plain (all-purpose) flour
filling
110g (3 oz) butter
200g (6 1/2 oz) brown sugar
2 tablespoons golden syrup
1/3 cup (2 3/4 fl oz) cream (single or pouring)

Preheat the oven to 160°C (315°F). Place the butter and sugar in the bowl of an electric mixer and beat until light and creamy. Add the flour and mix until combined.
Place tablespoonfuls of the mixture on baking trays lined with non-stick baking paper. Bake for 15 minutes or until golden. Allow to cool on a wire rack.
To make the filling, place the butter, sugar, golden syrup and cream in a saucepan over low heat and mix until smooth. Allow the caramel to simmer for 5 minutes or until thickened slightly.
Place the caramel in the fridge for 1 1/2 hours or until firm. Spread the caramel over half of the biscuits and sandwich together with the remaining biscuits. Serve with short black coffee. Makes 30 filled biscuits.

chocolate and peach panforte

caramel melting moments

espresso syrup cakes

menu ideas

breakfast for 2

parchment blueberry and passionfruit muffins
espresso granita

FOOD PREP
To be organised for an early morning start, prepare the parchment paper cylinders and measure the ingredients the night before, then mix the ingredients and bake the muffins in the morning.

LIQUID SUGGESTIONS
Ice-cold sparkling spring water with a wedge of lime and a few mint leaves is a great wake-up drink. Try freezing chopped fruit the night before, then, in the morning, putting it in a blender with a splash of juice and blending until smooth. For hot summer mornings, serve espresso granita instead of hot coffee. Freeze the granita the night before.

coffee and a chat for 8

little nectarine cakes
chocolate shortbread sandwiches
après café

FOOD PREP
Bake the chocolate shortbreads the day before and store in an airtight container. Fill the shortbreads and sandwich them together 30 minutes before serving. The little nectarine cakes are best made the day of serving. If nectarines are unavailable, use slices of fresh green apple or pear instead.

LIQUID SUGGESTIONS
If it's a mid-morning get-together, serve small bowls of après café (double the recipe) or freshly squeezed ruby grapefruit juice over sparkling mineral water.
For a lengthy afternoon session, I suggest starting with a sweet sparkling wine before coffee. For the brave, or for those who would rather sit back and listen, a shot of grappa or pastis with a little iced water may help your concentration.

post-dinner party for 6

chocolate and peach panforte
coconut and golden syrup wafers
espresso shots

FOOD PREP
Make the chocolate and peach panforte up to 2 days ahead of time and store in an airtight container. The coconut and golden syrup wafers can be made a day ahead and stored in an airtight container once completely cooled.

LIQUID SUGGESTIONS
Smooth espresso shots (which need to be made ahead of time) and a late-harvest or botrytis-affected riesling, well chilled, will hit the spot. Or be daring and go with a well-aged liqueur muscat or liqueur tokay.

coffee party for 12

espresso syrup cakes
caramel melting moments
little nectarine cakes
frozen caffè latte

FOOD PREP
Instead of dinner, throw a coffee party for a change. The espresso syrup cakes can be made ahead of time and warmed with their syrup. Bake the little nectarine cakes in small muffin tins for a shorter cooking time and smaller cakes, so guests can sample all the goodies. Bake the biscuits for the caramel melting moments the day before and store in an airtight container. Spread the biscuits with the caramel filling and sandwich together an hour before serving.

LIQUID SUGGESTIONS
If it is summer, serve frozen caffè lattes. For a large crowd, make large plungers or French presses of coffee or have somebody at the home espresso machine—whatever you do, don't reheat coffee. For more serious liquids, a botrytis-affected semillon or riesling, or a good aged port will work well with the coffee and the sweet cakes.

asian steaming

2

basics

utensils

BAMBOO STEAMERS come in a variety of sizes. Buy two steamers with a tight-fitting lid, which fit on top of each other over a wok, or buy smaller steamers that fit over your saucepans. Soak new steamers in cold water for 2 hours before using them. Oil the bases of the steamers or line them with non-stick baking paper to prevent food from sticking.

STRAINER, with its long bamboo handle, is great for removing fried foods from the wok or for draining foods.

CHOPSTICKS are great for picking up pieces of Asian food, noodles and sushi. They are also good for stirring ingredients and for placing across a wok to support a steamer.

SUSHI MAT is an essential inexpensive bamboo mat used to roll sushi rice and nori rolls.

wok, chan and brush

WOKS are ideal for cooking Asian-style food. Purchase a steel wok with a rounded base. Wash your wok well and season it before using by heating 2 tablespoons of oil over high heat until it is almost smoking. Brush the oil over the inside of the wok, allow the wok to cool and repeat this process three times or until the wok has a coating. Oil the wok before storing so it does not rust.

WOK SPOON OR CHAN is great for tossing and lifting ingredients in a wok.

WOK BRUSH is a stiff bamboo brush used to clean your wok with minimal effort. It will not scratch the seasoned surface of the wok. After cleaning, place the wok over high heat to dry.

sauces

SOY SAUCE ranges from light to dark and from sweet to salty. There are many different varieties. A good rule is: Chinese soy with Chinese food and Japanese soy with Japanese food. When using soy sauce, check the finished dish before serving. If the soy sauce you have used was too salty, add some shaved, crumbled palm sugar to reduce the saltiness.

OYSTER SAUCE is a fragrant, viscous sauce with oyster/seafood flavours. Buy good-quality oyster sauce that contains premium oyster extract.

FISH SAUCE is the clear amber liquid that drains from small fish that have been packed in wooden barrels with salt and fermented. Once you get past the aroma, the flavour becomes quite addictive.

PONZU is a great Japanese soy- and citrus-based sauce. Use it to marinate fish, seafood, meats and chicken. It also makes a great dipping sauce and is available at Asian grocers.

Asian greens

BOK CHOY has bright green leaves and pale green stems. The leaves and stems join to form a neat bunch. It is also available as baby bok choy and known as Chinese chard or Chinese white cabbage.

CHOY SUM, with thin, even, crisp stems, bright green leaves and, often, yellow flowers, is great to steam or stir-fry. Also known as Chinese flowering cabbage.

SNOW PEA SHOOTS are small, tender young shoots from the snow pea (mange tout) vine and have the same flavour as snow peas only a little milder. They are great in salads or stir-fries.

GAI LARN, also known as Chinese broccoli or Chinese kale, has stems that resemble broccoli stems. It produces white flowers. The stems, leaves and flowers are edible, and leave a slightly bitter aftertaste.

essential ingredients

PALM SUGAR is made from the sap of a palm tree. Usually, the darker the sugar is, the better it is. Shave fine slices off the block with a knife or vegetable peeler. It is used to balance saltiness and to flavour sweets.

TAMARIND can be purchased as a soft, dried pulp from the tamarind bean. The stringy pulp and seeds need to be soaked in hot water and stirred with a fork or squeezed with your fingers to release the flavour.

MIRIN is cooking wine made from rice. Purchase pure (hon) mirin. Japanese rice vinegar is a must for the sushi rice* lover. Steer away from the seasoned one, as it contains msg (monosodium glutamate).

CHILLI JAM is sold under many different names, including chilli paste with soy bean oil. It is a combination of chillies, fish sauce, shrimp paste, tamarind and shallots. Use it in cooking or as a dipping sauce.

SHAO HSING RICE WINE is Chinese cooking wine. Sweet sherry makes a good substitute.

Asian herbs

VIETNAMESE MINT, with long, pointed leaves, has a distinctive spicy and slightly bitter, but refreshing, flavour.

KAFFIR LIME LEAVES look like two leaves joined together like a butterfly. They have a distinctive citrus smell and a wonderful flavour. Simmer them whole in dishes or shred them finely.

THAI BASIL has a sweeter flavour than Italian basil. It has purple stems and, often, purple veins running through its leaves.

sushi mat

bamboo steamers

wok, brush and chan

strainers

chopsticks

33

sauces

fish sauce and oyster sauce

palm sugar

tamarind pulp and chilli jam

shao hsing wine, rice vinegar and mirin

kaffir lime leaves

gai larn

choy sum

snow pea shoots

bok choy

Thai basil

Vietnamese mint

prawn and chilli pot-sticker dumplings

vinegared rice box with marinated sashimi

pork rice noodle rolls

spinach with sesame and soy

vinegared rice box with marinated sashimi

250g (8 oz) sashimi tuna, sliced
250g (8 oz) sashimi salmon, sliced
1 quantity sushi rice*
2 tablespoons Japanese rice vinegar
marinade
3 tablespoons soy sauce
1 tablespoon lemon juice
2 teaspoons black sesame seeds*
2 tablespoons mirin
1 teaspoon wasabi* paste
2 tablespoons bonito flakes*

To make the marinade, place the soy sauce, lemon juice, sesame seeds, mirin, wasabi and bonito flakes in a non-reactive bowl*. Allow to stand for 2 hours, then strain. Place the marinade in a large shallow dish and add the tuna and salmon. The marinade should only cover the base of the sashimi. Allow to marinate for 10 minutes. Place the rice in 4 serving boxes and sprinkle with the rice vinegar. Top with pieces of sashimi and serve the marinade as a dipping sauce. Serve with pickled ginger, extra wasabi and soy sauce. Serves 6 as a starter, or 4 as a main.

prawn and chilli pot-sticker dumplings

500g (1 lb) green (raw) prawn (shrimp) meat, finely chopped
2 green onions (scallions), chopped
1 tablespoon shredded galangal* or ginger
1 tablespoon chopped coriander (cilantro)
1 tablespoon chilli jam
2 tablespoons Chinese cooking (shao hsing) wine
1 tablespoon soy sauce
30 round wonton wrappers*
1 tablespoon cornflour (cornstarch)
2 tablespoons water
1 tablespoon oil
1 cup (8 fl oz) vegetable* or fish stock*

Combine the prawns, onions, galangal, coriander, chilli jam, wine and soy sauce in a bowl. Place 1 tablespoonful of the mixture on each wonton wrapper. Mix the cornflour and water to a smooth paste and use to brush the edges of the wonton wrappers. Fold in half, gather up the edges like a fan and squeeze with your fingertips to enclose the filling. Heat the oil in a frying pan over high heat. Add the dumplings and cook the bases until golden. Add the stock and cover the pan. Allow the dumplings to steam for 3–4 minutes or until tender. Remove the lid and allow the stock to evaporate. Ensure the base of the dumplings is crisp. Serve immediately with extra chilli jam. Makes 30.

pork rice noodle rolls

300g (10 oz) fresh plain rice noodle rolls or flat rice noodles
filling
400g (13 oz) pork mince
1 red chilli, seeded and chopped
2 teaspoons finely chopped ginger
1 clove garlic, crushed
2 tablespoons chopped coriander (cilantro)
2 tablespoons soy sauce
dipping sauce
3 tablespoons hoisin sauce*
2 tablespoons Chinese cooking (shao hsing) wine
2 teaspoons chopped ginger

Soak the rice noodles in hot water until soft and pliable. To make the filling, place the pork, chilli, ginger, garlic, coriander and soy sauce in a bowl and mix well to combine. Take 1/3 cup of filling and roll it into a long sausage to fit the rice noodle rolls. Place some of the filling at the end of a flat rice noodle and roll up to enclose. Repeat using the remaining filling and rolls.
Place the rolls on a plate in a steamer and steam over a saucepan of boiling water for 5–6 minutes or until the filling is cooked through.
To make the dipping sauce, place the hoisin sauce, wine and ginger in a saucepan and heat until simmering. Pour into small bowls and serve with the pork rolls. Serves 4–6 as a starter.

spinach with sesame and soy

500g (1 lb) English spinach leaves
sesame dressing
1/3 cup sesame seeds
4 tablespoons soy sauce
1 tablespoon sugar
4 tablespoons mirin

Place the spinach in a saucepan of boiling water and cook for 10–15 seconds. Drain and place under cold running water to cool.
To make the sesame dressing, place the sesame seeds in a dry frying pan and toast until golden. Place the sesame seeds and 1 tablespoon of the soy sauce in a mortar and crush with the pestle to a smooth paste. Add the remaining soy sauce, sugar and mirin and mix to combine. Place in a small saucepan over medium heat and bring to the boil. Simmer for 2 minutes or until the dressing thickens.
Place the spinach on a serving plate and top with the sesame dressing. Sprinkle with extra sesame seeds and serve. Serves 4 as a starter or side dish.

rice noodles with barbecue duck

agedashi tofu

lemon-steamed chicken salad

red miso simmered eggplant

rice noodles with barbecue duck

1 Chinese barbecue duck*
400g (13 oz) fresh flat rice noodles
2 teaspoons sesame oil
1 tablespoon oil
1 tablespoon shredded ginger
10 green onions (scallions), cut into quarters
300g (10 oz) baby bok choy, broken into leaves
1/2 cup (4 fl oz) chicken stock*
2 tablespoons soy sauce
1/4 cup (2 fl oz) Chinese cooking (shao hsing) wine or sherry

Chop the duck into bite-sized pieces and remove as many bones as possible. Cut the rice noodles into very wide strips and rinse under hot water. Heat the oils in a wok or frying pan. Add the ginger and onions and cook for 1 minute. Add the duck and cook for 1 minute. Add the bok choy, rice noodles, stock, soy sauce and wine, and cook for 3–4 minutes or until the duck is heated through. Serves 4.

agedashi tofu

500g (1 lb) firm silken tofu, sliced
rice flour for dusting
oil for deep-frying
1 sheet nori,* finely shredded
sauce
1 1/2 cups (12 fl oz) dashi broth*
2 tablespoons soy sauce
3 tablespoons mirin
1 teaspoon sugar
8 small fresh shiitake mushrooms*
1 green onion (scallion), finely sliced

To make the sauce, place the dashi broth, soy sauce, mirin, sugar and mushrooms in a saucepan over low heat and allow to simmer for 3 minutes. Stir through the onion. Toss the tofu lightly in the rice flour and shake away any excess. Heat the oil in a saucepan over high heat. When the oil is hot, deep-fry the tofu, a few pieces at a time, until golden. Drain on paper towel.
To serve, place the hot tofu in bowls and pour over the sauce. Top with shredded nori and serve immediately. Serves 4–6 as a starter.

lemon-steamed chicken salad

2 lemons, sliced
4 chicken breast fillets
1 teaspoon Szechwan peppercorns,* roasted and crushed
salad
2 tablespoons Vietnamese mint, shredded
1/2 cup mint leaves
1/2 cup Thai basil leaves
100g (3 1/2 oz) snow pea (mange tout) shoots
2 red onions, finely sliced
2 red chillies, seeded and sliced
3 tablespoons lemon juice
2 tablespoons fish sauce
1 tablespoon palm or brown sugar
1 tablespoon soy sauce

Line a bamboo steamer with the lemon slices. Top with the chicken and sprinkle with the Szechwan peppercorns. Cover, place the steamer over a saucepan of boiling water and cook for 3–5 minutes or until the chicken is tender. Set aside to cool. Shred the chicken into fine pieces with your fingers.
To make the salad, combine the mints, basil, snow pea shoots, onions and chillies in a large serving bowl. Place the lemon juice, fish sauce, sugar and soy sauce in a small bowl and whisk to combine. Toss the chicken and dressing through the salad and serve. Serves 4.

red miso-simmered eggplant

2–3 tablespoons oil
2 eggplants (aubergines), chopped
2 teaspoons finely shredded ginger
2 tablespoons red miso*
2 tablespoons soy sauce
2 tablespoons mirin
1 1/2 cups (12 fl oz) dashi broth*

Heat the oil in a frying pan or wok and cook the eggplant pieces, a few at a time, until golden on both sides. Remove from the pan and set aside.
Add the ginger to the frying pan and cook for 1 minute. Add the miso, soy sauce, mirin and dashi broth and bring to the boil. Add the eggplant and allow to simmer for 4 minutes or until soft and the sauce has thickened. Serves 4 as a starter or side dish.

seared beef with soba

rice paper wrapped fish

wok-fried chicken with tamarind

seared beef with soba

500g (1 lb) eye fillet
noodles and broth
300g (10 oz) green tea soba noodles*
1 cup (8 fl oz) water
2 tablespoons soy sauce
3 tablespoons mirin
1 tablespoon sugar
2 tablespoons bonito flakes*
3 green onions (scallions), chopped
marinade
3 tablespoons soy sauce
1 tablespoon lemon juice
1 tablespoon mirin
2 teaspoons sesame oil

To cook the noodles, place in a large saucepan of boiling water and stir. Allow the water to come back to the boil and add 1 cup (8 fl oz) cold water. Repeat this process 3 times or until the noodles are soft. Drain and rinse the noodles well under cold running water.

To make the broth, place the water, soy sauce, mirin and sugar in a saucepan and bring to the boil. Add the bonito flakes and remove the pan from the heat. Set aside for 5 minutes. Strain the mixture through a fine sieve.

To make the marinade, combine the soy sauce, lemon juice, mirin and sesame oil. Pour over the beef and allow to marinate for 20 minutes.

To serve, toss the noodles in the strained broth and onions. Place on serving plates. Cook the beef on a hot grill (broiler) or frying pan for 1 minute on each side or until seared and warm inside. Slice the beef thinly and place on top of the noodles. Serves 4.

wok-fried chicken with tamarind

50g (1¾ oz) piece tamarind pulp
1 cup (8 fl oz) boiling water
2 double chicken breasts (850g or 1 lb 11 oz) on the bone
3 tablespoons soy sauce
1 tablespoon sesame oil
rice flour for dusting
2 tablespoons vegetable oil
8 green onions (scallions), halved
1 tablespoon shredded ginger
1 cup (8 fl oz) chicken stock*
2 tablespoons oyster sauce
1 tablespoon palm sugar

Place the tamarind pulp in a bowl and cover with the boiling water. Mix well with a fork to release the tamarind flavour and allow to stand for 5 minutes. Strain through a fine sieve. Cut the chicken into pieces. Place the soy sauce and sesame oil in a bowl and mix to combine. Add the chicken and allow to marinate for 30 minutes. Reserve the marinade. Toss the chicken in rice flour and shake off any excess. Heat the vegetable oil in a frying pan or wok over high heat. Cook the chicken, a few pieces at a time, until well browned. Set aside.

Add the reserved marinade, onions and ginger to the pan and cook for 1 minute. Add the stock, tamarind water, oyster sauce and sugar. Bring the sauce to the boil and simmer until reduced by half. Return the chicken to the pan and simmer for 4–5 minutes or until cooked through. Serve the chicken on plates with ready-made Chinese steamed buns■ and steamed greens. Serves 4.

■ Chinese buns, ready to steam, are available in the freezer section of Asian grocery stores.

rice paper wrapped fish

800g (1 lb 10 oz) piece blue eye cod fillet
2 green chillies, chopped
1 tablespoon sesame oil
4 tablespoons chopped coriander (cilantro)
2 tablespoons chopped Thai basil
1 teaspoon cumin seeds
12 large rice paper rounds*
oil for frying
black sesame seeds*

Wash the fish, pat dry on paper towel and cut into 12 pieces. Place the chillies, sesame oil, coriander, Thai basil and cumin seeds in a spice grinder or mortar and pestle and grind to a rough paste. Spread over the fish. Brush the rice paper rounds with warm water and set aside for 4 minutes or until soft. Place a piece of fish on each round, fold in the sides and roll to enclose.
Heat a little oil in a frying pan over medium heat. Cook the fish parcels for 2–3 minutes on each side or until the rice paper is golden and crisp, and the fish is tender. Drain on paper towels. Sprinkle with the sesame seeds. Serve with steamed Asian greens drizzled with oyster sauce and steamed jasmine rice. Serves 4.

tea cup steamed coconut cakes

4 eggs
1/2 cup sugar
1/4 cup grated palm sugar
1 tablespoon boiling water
1 1/4 cups plain (all-purpose) flour
1 1/4 teaspoons baking powder
3 tablespoons desiccated coconut

Place the eggs and sugar in the bowl of an electric mixer. Place the palm sugar and water in a bowl and mix until the sugar is dissolved. Add to the eggs and sugar. Beat the mixture at high speed for 8–10 minutes or until light and thick. Carefully fold through the flour, baking powder and coconut.
Spoon the mixture into 6 Chinese tea cups or small rice bowls. Place in a steamer over a wok of boiling water, cover and steam for 15 minutes or until the cakes are puffed and firm. Serve with small pots of Chinese tea. Makes 6.

sticky rice with mango and lime

1 cup glutinous rice*
2 1/2 cups (20 fl oz) water
1/2 cup (4 fl oz) coconut cream
3 tablespoons sugar
6 x 15cm (6 in) squares banana leaves
filling
1 mango, peeled and chopped
1 teaspoon grated lime rind
2 tablespoons lime juice
1 tablespoon grated palm sugar

Rinse the rice well under cold water and drain. Place the rice and water in a saucepan over medium heat and bring to the boil. Allow to simmer until almost all the liquid has been absorbed. Remove the pan from the heat and pour the coconut cream over the rice. Cover and allow to stand for 5–7 minutes or until the coconut cream has been absorbed. Stir the sugar through the rice and set aside. Place the banana leaves in boiling water for 1–2 minutes or until soft. Divide the rice into 6 portions. Spread half of each portion over the middle of a banana leaf. Top the rice with a sprinkling of mango, lime rind and juice, and palm sugar. Cover the filling with the remaining portion of rice. Roll up the leaves and secure with toothpicks. Place the leaf packages on a hot barbecue or char grill (broiler) and cook for 2 minutes on each side or until the rice is heated through. Serve warm or cold. Serves 6.

steamed palm sugar custards

1 cup (8 fl oz) milk
2 cups (16 fl oz) cream (single or pouring)
1/2 cup grated dark palm sugar
1 star anise
1 cinnamon stick
4 eggs

Place the milk, cream, sugar, star anise and cinnamon in a saucepan over low heat and cook for 5 minutes. Strain the mixture and place in a bowl. Beat the eggs lightly and whisk into the milk mixture.
Pour the mixture into 6–8 Chinese tea cups and place in a steamer. Place the steamer over rapidly simmering water and steam for 25 minutes or until the custards are just set. Serves 6–8.

tea cup steamed coconut cakes

sticky rice with mango and lime

steamed palm sugar custards

menu ideas

dim sum lunch for 6

pork rice noodle rolls
prawn and chilli pot-sticker dumplings
rice paper wrapped fish
rice noodles with Chinese barbecue duck
tea cup steamed coconut cakes

FOOD PREP
For starters, serve the pork rice noodle rolls and the prawn and chilli pot-sticker dumplings with bowls of chilli jam on the side. Both of these can be prepared ahead of time and steamed when required. For mains, serve the rice paper wrapped fish, which you can prepare beforehand and cook just before serving, and small bowls of the rice noodles with barbecue duck*. Finish with the tea cup steamed coconut cakes, which can be made a day in advance and refrigerated until required.

LIQUID SUGGESTIONS
The obvious choice would be a pot of Chinese tea such as jasmine or chrysanthemum tea. If you wish to drink wine, choose a young riesling to complement the chilli and spice.

Japanese dinner for 6

agedashi tofu
spinach with sesame and soy
vinegared rice box with marinated sashimi
seared beef with soba
sticky rice with mango and lime

FOOD PREP
Start with the well-flavoured agedashi tofu and the spinach with sesame and soy (double the recipe). The spinach can be prepared a few hours beforehand. Move on to the vinegared rice boxes with marinated sashimi (double the recipe) and the seared beef with soba (double the recipe). Remember to allow time for the sashimi marinade to stand. Even though sticky rice with mango and lime is not a Japanese dish, it will go well with the other dishes and you can make it beforehand and steam it when required. If time is short, serve ready-made green tea ice cream (available from Asian food stores).

LIQUID SUGGESTIONS
A warmed or chilled sake would work well. Check whether the sake you are buying is for drinking warm or chilled. You could also serve Japanese green tea or a dry Japanese beer.

Asian banquet for 8

spinach with sesame and soy
red miso-simmered eggplant
lemon-steamed chicken salad
seared beef with soba
steamed palm sugar custards

FOOD PREP
Start with a few dishes such as the spinach with sesame and soy (double the recipe), which is easily prepared a few hours beforehand, and the red miso*-simmered eggplant (aubergine) (double the recipe). Prepare the lemon-steamed chicken salad and refrigerate until required, and serve it with the seared beef with soba. Finish with the velvety steamed palm sugar custards, which can be steamed a day in advance and refrigerated until you are ready to serve.

LIQUID SUGGESTIONS
A big pot of Chinese tea would be great. This menu also suits a cold dry beer, a riesling or a sauvignon blanc.

morsels with drinks for 10

spinach with sesame and soy
agedashi tofu
prawn and chilli pot-sticker dumplings
rice paper wrapped fish
lemon-steamed chicken salad

FOOD PREP
The spinach with sesame and soy and the agedashi tofu can be served in Chinese soup spoons. Both can be prepared ahead of time. Deep-fry the tofu just before serving. Serve the dumplings on a platter with small bowls of chilli jam. The rice paper wrapped fish can be made into smaller bite-sized pieces and the lemon-steamed chicken salad can be served in individual baby cos (romaine) lettuce leaves.

LIQUID SUGGESTIONS
Serve small bottles of chilled sake or shot glasses of warm sake. See drinks chapter (page 100) for cocktail suggestions.

garden
lunch

3

basics

Fruits, vegetables and herbs are best purchased, cooked and eaten when they are in season. At the height of their season, they have the maximum flavour and are probably at their best price. Growing seasons are being extended all the time with new varieties of fruits and vegetables and, with the help of modern transport, seasonal produce is often available for longer periods. Use the following loose guide for a few of your favourites.

any time

As a result of advanced growing techniques, many more fruits and vegetables are available year round. These include beetroots (beets), capsicums (bell peppers), eggplants (aubergines) and sweet potatoes (kumara).

summer

From the heady aroma of basil to succulent stone fruits, summer is the perfect time for the fruit and berry lover. To prolong your enjoyment of summer stone fruits, preserve them in a light sugar syrup or make them into jams and chutneys for the colder months ahead. Summer favourites include basil, berries, corn, cucumbers, figs, garlic, lettuce, peas, new potatoes, salad greens, snake beans, stone fruits, tomatoes and zucchini (courgettes).

spring

The season for an amazing variety of delicate green vegetables. Lightly blanch tender young spring greens for simple, fresh salads. Spring produce includes Asian greens, asparagus, beans, broad (fava) beans, carrots, globe artichokes, peas, rocket (árugula) and spinach.

autumn

Autumn, the mellow season, is a time to prepare for the colder months. Warming pasta dishes and risotto help the transition to winter. Try mushrooms, okra, olives, onions, pumpkin and spinach during autumn.

winter

Winter is a great time for soups and slowly simmered dishes that contain hearty root vegetables and winter-cropping members of the brassica family. Look out for blood oranges, broccoli, Brussels sprouts, cabbage, cauliflower, celeriac (celery root), fennel, Jerusalem artichokes, leeks, parsnips, potatoes, persimmons and quinces during the winter months.

any time

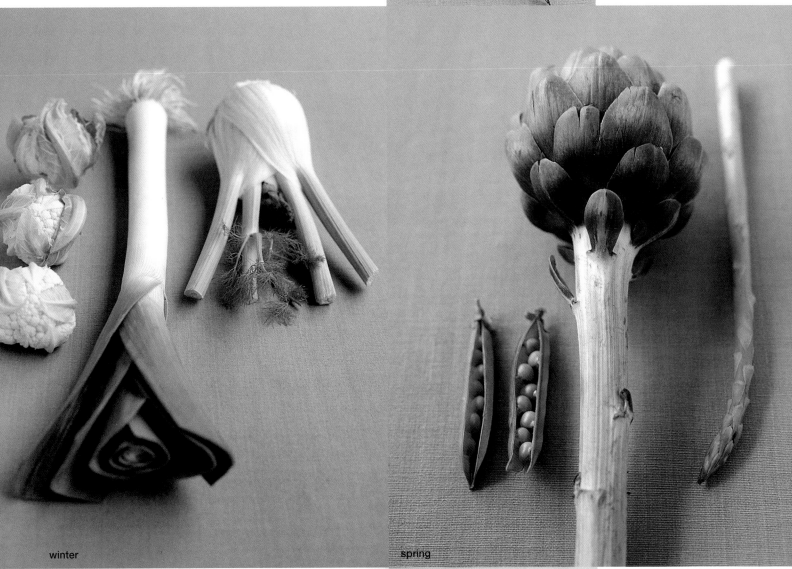

winter

spring

autumn

summer

marinated sheep's yoghurt cheese

fennel and mushroom salad

marinated beets   seared scallops on lemon and mint salad

marinated sheep's yoghurt cheese

1kg (2 lb) sheep's milk yoghurt
1 tablespoon sea salt
2 teaspoons cracked black pepper
2 tablespoons chopped lemon thyme
1 red chilli, seeded and chopped

Combine the yoghurt, salt, pepper, lemon thyme and chilli. Pour into a bowl lined with a double layer of cheesecloth. Tie the ends of the cheesecloth together and suspend the bundle from a shelf in the fridge over a bowl, to collect the drips, for 24–48 hours or until the yoghurt mixture is firm.
Remove the yoghurt from the cheesecloth and shape it into small balls. Place on a tray, cover loosely and refrigerate for 3–4 hours or until the yoghurt balls become firm. Slice the balls and serve on grilled bread. Use within 3 days or store the cheese balls whole, covered in olive oil, in a sterilised jar* in the fridge. Makes 10 balls.

fennel and mushroom salad

4 large field mushrooms
2 tablespoons butter, melted
1 tablespoon oil
150g (5 oz) baby English spinach leaves
1 tablespoon sage leaves
1 tablespoon shredded lemon rind
2 baby fennel bulbs, thinly sliced
1/2 cup marinated green olives
cracked black pepper
2 tablespoons balsamic vinegar

Wipe the mushrooms clean and trim the stems. Brush with the butter and oil and place on a preheated hot grill (broiler). Cook for 2 minutes each side.
To serve, place a pile of baby spinach leaves on each plate. Scatter over the sage leaves and lemon rind and top with a mushroom. Top with the fennel, olives and pepper. Drizzle the balsamic vinegar over the salad and serve with warm sourdough bread. Serves 4 as a starter.

marinated beets

18 baby beetroots (beets), peeled and trimmed
2 cups (16 fl oz) white wine vinegar
1 cup (8 fl oz) water
1/2 cup sugar
1 tablespoon coriander seeds
2 tablespoons orange rind strips
2 tablespoons dill sprigs

Place the beetroots in a saucepan of boiling water and cook for 6 minutes or until tender. Drain and peel. Place the vinegar, water, sugar, coriander seeds and orange rind strips in a non-reactive saucepan* and bring to the boil. Remove the pan from the heat and add the beetroot and dill. Allow the mixture to cool. Store the beetroot and marinade in sterilised jars* in the fridge. Serve with washed-rind cheese and bread. Makes 1 medium jar.

seared scallops on lemon and mint salad

24 scallops
cracked black pepper
olive oil
2 teaspoons grated lemon rind
salad
2 cups mint leaves
1/2 cup Vietnamese mint leaves
1 bunch (100g or 31/2 oz) rocket (arugula) leaves
1/4 cup (2 fl oz) lemon juice
1 red chilli, seeded and chopped
2 teaspoons grated ginger
1 tablespoon vegetable oil

Combine the scallops with a little pepper and oil and the lemon rind. Set aside for 5 minutes.
Combine the mints and rocket and arrange on plates.
Combine the lemon juice, chilli, ginger and oil.
Place a frying pan over high heat. Add the scallops and cook for 10 seconds each side or until seared. Place the scallops on the salad and pour over the lemon dressing. Serves 4 to 6 as a starter.

pickled spring onions

24 small brown or spring pickling onions
5 cups (40 fl oz) white wine vinegar
6 tablespoons sugar
1 teaspoon cumin seeds
8 sprigs dill
4 sprigs marjoram
4 red chillies, halved and seeds removed
1 teaspoon black peppercorns

Peel and trim the onions and set aside. Place the vinegar and sugar in a non-reactive saucepan* and bring to the boil. Once the vinegar boils, add the onions, cumin seeds, dill, marjoram, chillies and peppercorns. Simmer for 6–8 minutes or until the onions are soft. Pour into a sterilised jar* and seal with a non-metallic lid. Allow the onions to stand for at least 2 days before serving. Makes 1 large jar.

parmesan and sorrel grilled witlof

4 witlof (chicory), halved
sea salt
1 cup young sorrel leaves
1/4 cup flat-leaf parsley
3 tablespoons lemon juice
1 tablespoon sugar
cracked black pepper
1/2 cup grated parmesan cheese

Bring a saucepan of water to the boil. Add the witlof and a little salt and cook for 4 minutes or until the witlof are tender. Drain well.
Place the sorrel and parsley leaves between the witlof leaves. Place on a baking tray and sprinkle with the lemon juice, sugar, pepper and parmesan. Place under a preheated hot grill (broiler) and cook for 4–6 minutes or until golden.
Serve with slices of smoked salmon and salad greens. Serves 4.

asparagus with herb brown butter sauce

750g (1 1/2 lb) asparagus, trimmed and halved
90g (3 oz) butter
cracked black pepper
2 tablespoons sage leaves
2 tablespoons oregano leaves
2 tablespoons marjoram leaves
1 tablespoon lemon juice
cooked pasta to serve
shaved parmesan to serve

Place the asparagus in a steamer or in boiling water and cook until tender. Drain.
To make the herb brown butter sauce, place the butter, pepper, sage, oregano and marjoram in a saucepan over medium heat and cook for 4–6 minutes or until the butter is golden brown. Remove from the heat and add the lemon juice.
Place a pile of pasta on each plate. Top with some asparagus. Spoon the herb brown butter over and serve with parmesan cheese. Serves 6 as a starter or 4 as a main meal.

pear, ginger and chilli chutney

1 kg (2 lb) pears, peeled, cored and chopped
1/4 cup shredded ginger
6 red chillies, seeded and chopped
2 onions, finely chopped
3 tablespoons chopped coriander (cilantro)
2 kaffir lime* leaves
2 1/2 cups (20 fl oz) cider vinegar
1 cup brown sugar
1 cup white sugar
sea salt and cracked black pepper

Place the pears, ginger, chillies, onions, coriander, kaffir lime leaves, vinegar and sugars in a non-reactive saucepan* over high heat. Bring to the boil, then reduce the heat to a simmer and cook for 30 minutes or until thick, stirring occasionally and skimming the surface. Taste the chutney before adding salt and pepper.
Pour into sterilised jars* and seal. Serve the chutney on sandwiches or with grilled or roast meats. Makes 1 large jar.

pickled spring onions

asparagus with herb brown butter sauce

parmesan and sorrel grilled witlof

pear, ginger and chilli chutney

59

green pea broth

filled tomatoes + (right) basil-rubbed toasts

green pea broth

2 smoked ham hocks, halved
3 litres (96 fl oz) water
1½ cups (12 fl oz) dry white wine
12 pearl or small brown onions
3 bay leaves
1 teaspoon peppercorns
2 cups fresh peas
1 cup shredded celeriac (celery root) or parsnip
1 tablespoon mint leaves
1 tablespoon chervil sprigs

Remove the skin and any visible fat from the hocks. Place in a large stockpot with the water, wine, onions, bay leaves and peppercorns. Bring to the boil, then cover and simmer for 1 hour. Strain the stock through a fine sieve. Remove the onions from the pot and wash and halve them. Chop the meat from the bones and place in a clean saucepan with the onions.
Add the stock to the pan and bring to the boil. Add the peas and celeriac and simmer for 5 minutes or until tender. Ladle the soup into bowls and sprinkle with the mint and chervil. Serve with grilled bread. Serves 4 to 6 as a starter.

filled tomatoes with basil-rubbed toasts

4 ripe beefsteak or garden tomatoes
4 bocconcini or 300g (10 oz) smoked mozzarella, sliced
⅓ cup shaved parmesan cheese
½ cup basil leaves
½ cup (4 fl oz) balsamic vinegar
3 tablespoons extra-virgin olive oil
2 teaspoons brown sugar
sea salt and cracked black pepper
mixed salad greens
basil-rubbed toasts
12 slices crusty Italian bread
olive oil
1 large bunch basil

Cut slits almost completely through the tomatoes, leaving the bases intact. Fill with the bocconcini or mozzarella, parmesan and basil. Combine the balsamic vinegar, olive oil, sugar, salt and pepper, and pour over the tomatoes. Allow to stand for at least 20 minutes.
To make the basil-rubbed toasts, brush the bread with the oil and toast under a griller (broiler) until golden brown on both sides. Take a large handful of the basil leaves and rub them into one side of the warm pieces of toast.
To serve, place the salad greens on plates and top with the tomatoes. Serve with the warm basil-rubbed toasts and lots of cracked pepper. Serves 4.

summer fruits free-form pie

1 quantity (350g or 12 oz) sweet shortcrust pastry*
milk
demerara sugar*
filling
2 peaches, sliced
200g (6½ oz) raspberries
3 plums, sliced
200g (6½ oz) blueberries
1 tablespoon plain (all-purpose) flour

Roll out the pastry on a lightly floured surface to 3mm (⅛ in) thick. Place in a 23cm (9 in) pie dish, leaving an 8–10cm (3–4 in) overhang. Refrigerate until required.
To make the filling, combine the peaches, raspberries, plums, blueberries and flour. Place in the pie base. Fold over the excess pastry to partly encase the fruit. Refrigerate for 20 minutes or until the pastry is firm. Preheat the oven to 200°C (400°F). Brush the pastry with a little milk and sprinkle generously with sugar.
Bake for 20 minutes or until the pastry is golden and the fruit is tender. Serve warm or cold with clotted cream. Serves 8 to 10.
Note: when making the pastry for this pie, use 30g (1 oz) less butter than given in the glossary and more iced water to make the pastry firmer.

sour lemon cake

125g (4 oz) butter
¾ cup caster (superfine) sugar
1½ tablespoons grated lemon rind
2 eggs, lightly beaten
1½ cups plain (all-purpose) flour
1½ teaspoons baking powder
½ cup sour cream
½ cup (4 fl oz) lemon juice

Preheat the oven to 180°C (350°F). Place the butter, sugar and lemon rind in the bowl of an electric mixer and beat until light and creamy. Add the eggs and beat well. Fold the flour, baking powder, sour cream and lemon juice through. Immediately place the mixture in a greased 20cm (8 in) square cake tin lined with non-stick baking paper and bake for 40 minutes or until the cake is cooked when tested with a skewer. Cut into wedges and serve warm with cream. Serves 8 to 10.

sour lemon cake

summer fruits free-form pie

menu ideas

sunday lunch for 4

marinated beets
seared scallops on lemon and mint salad
summer fruits free-form pie

FOOD PREP
Prepare the marinated beets up to 3–4 days before serving with washed-rind cheese and crusty bread. Follow this with the scallop salad. Prepare the salad the morning before serving and sear the scallops just before serving. Serve the summer fruits free-form pie for dessert with clotted cream. The pie can be made in the morning before your guests arrive.

LIQUID SUGGESTIONS
Serve an aged semillon or chardonnay with the beets. The flavour of the scallops would be good with a semillon or sauvignon blanc. Serve the pie with your choice of sweet wine or a lazy-afternoon glass of port and a cup of coffee.

mezze lunch for 6

marinated beets
marinated sheep's yoghurt cheese
pickled spring onions
parmesan and sorrel grilled witlof
seared scallops on lemon and mint salad
sour lemon cake

FOOD PREP
Most of this lunch can be prepared well in advance. Have a large table layed out with the marinated beets, yoghurt cheese, pickled onions, grilled witlof (chicory) and a platter of scallops on lemon and mint salad. This allows people to pick and choose. Be sure to serve plenty of bread and some extra cheeses to round out the table. Make the lemon cake the day before and store in an airtight container. When you are ready to serve, cut it into wedges and serve with thick cream, to complete a perfect lunch.

LIQUID SUGGESTIONS
With all the full-flavoured marinated goodies, serve a lightly wooded chardonnay as your white wine and a well-flavoured pinot noir as your red. The cake is a treat with an apple- or pear-infused brandy and strong coffee.

light spring lunch for 8

fennel and mushroom salad
asparagus with herb brown butter sauce

FOOD PREP
Start with the fennel and mushroom salad (double the recipe) with some flatbreads on the side. Follow this with the asparagus with herb brown butter sauce (double the recipe) nestled on a mound of chilli pasta. For dessert, serve a plate of fresh fruits sprinkled with lime and palm sugar or a drizzle of botrytis-affected riesling.

LIQUID SUGGESTIONS
Try sparkling spring water flavoured with lemon thyme and lime wedges or a fresh fruit cordial (see portable food). If wine is your wish, a crisp sauvignon blanc would be perfect.

formal garden lunch for 10

green pea broth
filled tomatoes with basil-rubbed toasts
asparagus with herb brown butter sauce
summer fruits free-form pie

FOOD PREP
Start with the green pea broth (double the recipe), which can be prepared ahead of time and gently warmed before serving. Then serve a starter of filled tomatoes with basil-rubbed toasts (double the recipe), which can be prepared a few hours beforehand. Follow these with asparagus with herb brown butter sauce (double the recipe) and finish with a summer fruits free-form pie with vanilla bean ice cream. Prepare the pastry for the pie the day before and refrigerate until you are ready to roll out the pastry and make the pie.

LIQUID SUGGESTIONS
A sparkling white wine, a refreshing riesling or a clean sauvignon blanc will suit the green pea broth and a chardonnay goes well with the tomatoes. Continue with the chardonnay or offer a spicy pinot noir with the asparagus. Accompany the pie with a chilled late-cut riesling and coffees.

grill 4

basics

There are many different sites where you can grill (broil) foods, from the traditional backyard barbecue to the grill (broiler) pan on your cooktop or the electric char grill. As there are now many indoor grilling options, this method of cooking is not only for the warm, fine-weather months. Indoor grilling is best done in a well-ventilated kitchen.

herb brushes

To avoid melting a normal kitchen basting brush, use a bunch of herbs tied with string to dip in the cooking oil and brush the grill (broiler) or barbecue. To reduce the amount of smoke from the grill (especially if you are grilling inside), brush the food not the grill. Use sturdy herbs such as rosemary, thyme, lemon thyme, oregano or marjoram.

barbecues

These come in many different varieties. Some have grills and flat plates combined with volcanic rocks, heat beads or coals. Woodchips or smoking chips are great for home smoking in covered barbecues. Barbecues are handy for cooking large fish and covered barbecues are great for large roasts. It'll keep the heat out of the kitchen during summer.

char grills

Electric char grills (broilers) or in-bench gas or electric grills are great alternatives to the backyard barbecue. When using these inside, remember to open the window or turn on the exhaust fan.

tongs

If you are grilling (broiling) a substantial amount of food over high heat, use long-handled tongs for flipping sausages, steaks, fish and burgers on the barbecue or grill. Avoid leaving tongs on a hot surface as they heat up quickly.

grill pans

These are great for use indoors, and they are sometimes more convenient than outdoor barbecues. Grill (broiler) pans come in flat-plate as well as frying pan varieties for use on the stove top. Flat-plate grills often cover two elements on the stove top, so check the size before purchasing one. They are mostly available in cast iron but a few are made of a lighter steel with a non-stick coating.

grill pan

char grill

herb brush

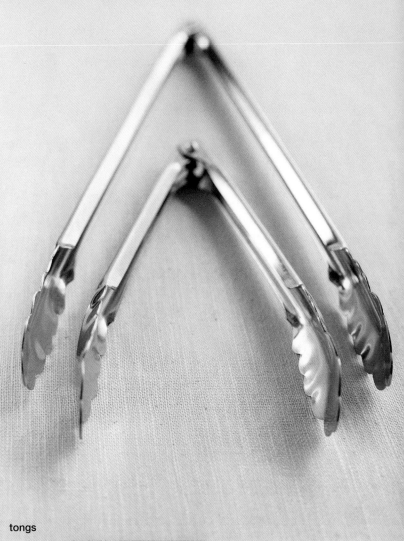
tongs

barbecue

smoked eggplant and white bean puree + rosemary and sea-salt grilled flatbreads

swordfish grilled with vine leaves

smoked eggplant and white bean puree

2 eggplants (aubergines)
2 cloves garlic, unpeeled
1 cup cooked cannellini beans
1/3 cup (2¾ fl oz) olive oil
1 tablespoon tahini
1/4 teaspoon ground cumin
1/4 cup (2 fl oz) lemon juice
2 tablespoons chopped flat-leaf parsley
1 tablespoon chopped mint
sea salt and cracked black pepper

Place the eggplants and garlic on a preheated hot grill (broiler) and cook for 6–8 minutes or until the skins are well charred and the flesh is soft. Peel the skins from the eggplant and garlic. Place the flesh in a food processor or blender with the beans, oil, tahini, cumin and lemon juice, and process until smooth.
Stir the parsley, mint, salt and pepper through the puree. Serve with warm grilled bread. Serves 6 to 8 as a starter.

grilled eggplant and mint salad

2 eggplants (aubergines), sliced
2 small fennel bulbs, sliced
2 zucchini (courgettes), sliced
olive oil
150g (5 oz) haloumi,* sliced
1/2 cup shredded mint
3 tablespoons lemon juice
2 tablespoons chopped flat-leaf parsley
1 tablespoon honey
cracked black pepper

Brush the eggplant, fennel and zucchini slices with a little oil. Place on a preheated hot grill (broiler) and grill for 1–2 minutes on each side or until the vegetables are soft. Brush the haloumi slices with a little oil. Place on a flat grill or in a hot frying pan and cook for 1 minute on each side or until golden.
Arrange the grilled vegetables and haloumi on plates and sprinkle with the mint. Combine the lemon juice, parsley, honey and pepper and pour over the salad. Serve with bread. Serves 4 to 6 as a starter.

swordfish grilled with vine leaves

4 swordfish steaks
2 teaspoons grated lemon rind
1 clove garlic, crushed
2 tablespoons finely chopped flat-leaf parsley
2 tablespoons olive oil
8 fresh vine leaves or leaves in brine
olive oil, extra

Trim the swordfish skin and wash and pat the fish dry. Combine the lemon rind, garlic, parsley and olive oil. Brush over both sides of the fish. Place a vine leaf on each side of the fish and tuck in the ends to secure. Brush with a little oil and place on a grill (broiler) tray. Place the tray under a hot grill and cook for 2–3 minutes on each side or until the fish is tender. Serve with a spinach salad and lemon wedges. Serves 4.

rosemary and sea-salt grilled flatbreads

1 teaspoon active dry yeast
2½ cups (20 fl oz) warm water
3½ cups wholemeal plain (all-purpose) flour
2 teaspoons sea salt
1 tablespoon olive oil
2½ –3 cups plain (all-purpose) flour
olive oil, extra
sea salt, extra
rosemary leaves

Place the yeast and water in a bowl and stir to combine. Place the wholemeal flour in the bowl of an electric mixer fitted with a dough hook. (Or use a bowl and wooden spoon.) Add the yeast mixture to the flour and mix until well combined. Cover with plastic wrap and allow to stand in a warm place for 1 hour or until the dough has doubled in size.
Add the salt and oil and beat with the dough hook until combined. While the motor is running, gradually add the plain flour until a soft dough forms. Allow the dough hook to knead the dough for 8 minutes. Cover with plastic wrap and allow to double in size (this takes about 2 hours). Divide the dough into 16 pieces and roll each piece into a ball. Roll out the balls on a lightly floured surface until 4mm (1/4 in) thick. Brush one side with a little olive oil, and sprinkle with some salt and rosemary leaves. Allow to rise for 10 minutes.
Cook the flatbreads on a preheated hot grill (broiler) or barbecue for 1 minute each side or until they are puffed and golden. Serve warm. Makes 16.

grilled eggplant and mint salad

spicy rocket and beef sausage

beef burgers with fried tomatoes and chillies

chilli salt and pepper squid

kaffir salmon with grilled limes

coriander prawns with honey bok choy

beef burgers with fried tomatoes and chillies

500g (1 lb) minced beef
2 tablespoons Worcestershire sauce
1 clove garlic, crushed
2 tablespoons Dijon mustard
2 tablespoons chopped coriander (cilantro)
1 onion, sliced
2 green tomatoes, sliced
2 mild green chillies, sliced
2 tablespoons oil
salad greens
4 bread rolls, halved and toasted

Combine the beef, Worcestershire sauce, garlic, mustard and coriander. Divide the mixture into 4 and shape into patties. Place the patties, onions, tomatoes and chillies on a preheated hot grill (broiler). Brush the oil over the onion, tomatoes and chillies. Cook for 3 minutes each side or until the vegetables are well browned and the patties are cooked through.
Place salad greens on the bottom half of the bread rolls. Top with the onions, patties, tomatoes and chillies. Cover with the top of the roll and serve. Serves 4.

spicy rocket and beef sausage

750g (1½ lb) sausage mince
250g (8 oz) minced beef
2 cups shredded rocket (arugula)
3 tablespoons seeded mustard
1 clove garlic, crushed
2 tablespoons chopped thyme
cracked black pepper
sausage skins■

Combine the sausage mince, minced beef, rocket, mustard, garlic, thyme and pepper. Place the mixture in a piping bag fitted with a large plain nozzle. Slide the sausage skin over the nozzle of the piping bag and gather the skin over the nozzle until you reach the end. Pipe the mixture into the sausage skin, allowing the skin to slide from the nozzle as you pipe. Twist the sausage at regular intervals to form individual sausages about 12–15cm (5–6 in) long. Place in the fridge for 4 hours or overnight.
To cook, place the sausages in a saucepan of cold water. Slowly bring the water to a simmer, then remove from the heat and drain the sausages. Cook the sausages on a preheated medium hot grill (broiler) or barbecue until cooked through. Serve with a spicy chutney and grilled onion. Serves 4 to 6.
■ Available from your butcher.

chilli salt and pepper squid

3 red chillies, seeded and chopped
1 tablespoon sea-salt flakes
1 teaspoon cracked black pepper
12 baby or small squid, cleaned and halved
2 tablespoons oil
100g (3½ oz) rice vermicelli
3 tablespoons soy sauce
2 tablespoons lime juice
3 tablespoons coriander (cilantro) leaves
1 tablespoon brown sugar
2 teaspoons fish sauce

Combine the chillies, salt and pepper in a bowl. Brush the squid lightly with the oil and press in the chilli mixture to coat both sides. Set aside.
Place the rice vermicelli in a bowl and pour over boiling water to cover. Allow to stand for 5 minutes or until the noodles are tender. Drain. Toss with the soy sauce, lime juice, coriander, sugar and fish sauce. Divide the vermicelli between bowls.
To cook the squid, preheat a grill (broiler) or frying pan over high heat. Cook the squid for 10–15 seconds on each side. Place on top of the vermicelli and serve. Serves 4.

kaffir salmon with grilled limes

4 kaffir lime* leaves, shredded
2 tablespoons lime juice
2 teaspoons grated ginger
2 teaspoons sesame oil
2 teaspoons chilli oil*
4 x 185g (6 oz) pieces salmon fillet
4 limes, halved
salad greens to serve

Combine the kaffir lime leaves, lime juice, ginger, and sesame and chilli oils. Pour over the salmon and allow to marinate for 10 minutes.
Place the salmon and limes, flesh-side down, on a preheated hot grill (broiler) and cook for 1 minute each side or until cooked to your liking. Serve the salmon with the grilled limes and salad greens tossed in a light lemon dressing. Serves 4.

balsamic marinated steak

herb chicken skewers

coriander prawns with honey bok choy

750g (1½ lb) large green (raw) prawns (shrimp)
¼ cup chopped coriander (cilantro)
2 tablespoons lime juice
2 teaspoons sesame oil
1 green chilli, seeded and chopped
1 tablespoon chopped mint
honey bok choy
400g (13 oz) baby bok choy (see page 32)
3 tablespoons honey
3 tablespoons Chinese cooking (shao hsing) wine
 (see page 32)
1 tablespoon sesame seeds
3 tablespoons oyster sauce

Remove the heads from the prawns, then peel and devein but leave the tails intact. Place each prawn on a skewer. Combine the coriander, lime juice, sesame oil, chilli and mint. Pour over the prawns and allow to marinate for at least 10 minutes.
To make the honey bok choy, place the bok choy in a saucepan of boiling water and cook for 30 seconds, then drain. Place the honey, wine, sesame seeds and oyster sauce in a frying pan over medium heat and allow to simmer. Add the bok choy and cook for 1 minute.
Place the prawns on a hot barbecue, char grill (broiler) or in a frying pan and cook for 1–2 minutes each side or until just cooked. To serve, place the bok choy on plates and top with the prawns. Serves 4 to 6 as a starter.

balsamic marinated steak

4 steaks (fillet, New York or Scotch fillet)
salad greens
marinade
⅓ cup (2¾ oz) balsamic vinegar
⅓ cup (2¾ oz) olive oil
2 tablespoons shredded basil
1 teaspoon cracked black pepper
2 pieces lemon rind, thinly sliced
2 cloves garlic, sliced

Trim the steak of excess fat. To make the marinade, combine the balsamic vinegar, oil, basil, pepper, lemon rind and garlic. Place the steak in the marinade and allow to marinate for at least 30 minutes.
To cook the steak, preheat a char grill (broiler), barbecue or frying pan over very high heat. Cook the steak until it is well sealed and cooked to your liking. To serve, pile the salad greens onto plates and top with the grilled steak. Serves 4.

herb chicken skewers

4 chicken breast fillets
¼ cup rosemary sprigs
¼ cup oregano sprigs
10 mild red chillies, halved and seeded
3 tablespoons lemon juice
3 tablespoons soy sauce
2 teaspoons sesame oil
2 cloves garlic, crushed
2 teaspoons grated ginger
1 tablespoon brown sugar

Cut the chicken into thick strips. Thread onto skewers with the sprigs of rosemary and oregano and the chillies. Combine the lemon juice, soy sauce, sesame oil, garlic, ginger and sugar. Pour over the chicken and allow to marinate for 20 minutes.
To cook, place the chicken skewers on a hot grill (broiler) and cook for 2 minutes each side or until cooked through. Serve with salad greens. Serves 4.

lemon and Szechwan pepper sardines

12 fresh sardines, butterflied
2 parsnips, peeled
oil for deep-frying
sea salt
marinade
3 tablespoons lemon juice
2 tablespoons Szechwan peppercorns,* toasted and crushed
2 tablespoons olive oil
2 tablespoons Thai basil (see page 32), shredded

Wash the sardines and pat dry. To make the marinade, combine the lemon juice, peppercorns, oil and basil. Pour over the sardines and allow to marinate for 20 minutes.
Cut the parsnips into thin strips. In a saucepan, heat the oil for deep-frying. Cook the parsnip strips, a few at a time, until golden and crisp. Drain on paper towel and keep warm in a warm oven.
To cook the sardines, preheat a grill (broiler), barbecue or frying pan over high heat. Cook the sardines for 1–2 minutes each side or until tender. To serve, place the parsnip chips on plates and top with salt and the sardines. Serves 4 as a starter.

lemon and szechwan pepper sardines

grill

tequila, lime and ruby grapefruit sorbet

grilled mango with coconut praline

tequila, lime and ruby grapefruit sorbet

1 cup (8 fl oz) lime juice
1 tablespoon finely grated lime rind
1 1/4 cups sugar
3 cups (24 fl oz) bottled ruby grapefruit juice
1/3 cup (2 3/4 fl oz) tequila

Place the lime juice, lime rind and sugar in a saucepan. Stir over low heat until the sugar is dissolved. Pour the ruby grapefruit juice, sugar mixture and tequila into a bowl and stir to combine. Pour the mixture into an ice-cream maker and follow the manufacturer's instructions to make sorbet. Alternatively, pour the mixture into a bowl and freeze for 1 hour. Whisk the sorbet and freeze for another hour. Whisk the sorbet again and freeze until solid. Serve in scoops. Serves 6.

pears with maple syrup and yoghurt

2 pears, sliced
60g (2 oz) butter, melted
1/3 cup demerara sugar*
1 cup thick yoghurt
1/4 cup (2 fl oz) maple syrup

Brush the pears with the butter and sprinkle with the sugar. Place the pear slices on a preheated hot flat grill (broiler) or frying pan and cook for 1 minute each side or until golden. To serve, stack slices of pear on plates. Top with a spoonful of yoghurt and drizzle with maple syrup. Serves 4.

grilled mango with coconut praline

2 mangoes
1 tablespoon lime juice
coconut praline
1 cup sugar
1/2 cup (4 fl oz) water
1 cup toasted shredded coconut

To make the coconut praline, place the sugar and water in a saucepan over low heat and stir until the sugar is dissolved. Allow the syrup to rapidly simmer for 5–7 minutes or until a light golden colour.
Spread the coconut on a baking tray and pour over the hot sugar mixture to cover. Allow to stand for 5 minutes or until the praline is hard. Break into small pieces.
Slice the cheeks from the mangoes and brush with lime juice. Place on a preheated hot grill (broiler), flesh-side down, and grill for 3 minutes or until golden and warm.
To serve, place the mango on plates with the coconut praline. Serves 4.

pears with maple syrup and yoghurt

menu ideas

barbecue for 8

chilli salt and pepper squid
herb chicken skewers
balsamic marinated steak
grilled eggplant and mint salad
tequila, lime and ruby grapefruit sorbet

FOOD PREP
Two dishes make a great informal starter: the chilli salt and pepper squid and the herb chicken skewers. Prepare these beforehand, without cooking, refrigerate and barbecue when required. Marinate the steaks (double the recipe) up to 2 hours before barbecuing, and the grilled eggplant and mint salad (double the recipe) can be prepared ahead of time too. Serve mains with a bowl of salad greens, and a selection of mustards and chutneys. Finish with the tequila, lime and ruby grapefruit sorbet, which can be made up to 2 days ahead.

LIQUID SUGGESTIONS
Lots of cold water, still or sparkling, is great when you are sitting around outdoors in the sun. Some say you can't really go past a good ice-cold beer at a barbecue, but if you can, try a riesling or sauvignon blanc with the starters and a cabernet sauvignon or well-flavoured, spicy chilled pinot noir with the steaks. For the wild at heart, a few cold shots of tequila with the sorbet won't go astray.

seaside dinner for 4

lemon and Szechwan pepper sardines
swordfish grilled with vine leaves
grilled mango with coconut praline

FOOD PREP
Start with the great textures and flavours of the lemon and Szechwan pepper sardines. Follow this with the swordfish grilled with vine leaves and some green salad leaves dressed in lemon and olive oil. The swordfish can be prepared ahead of time and barbecued when required. Finish with the grilled mango with coconut praline. You can make the coconut praline ahead of time and store it in an airtight container away from moisture.

LIQUID SUGGESTIONS
Fruit- and herb-infused mineral waters are nice to start with. The rich sardines are great with an aged semillon or lightly wooded chardonnay. Stick to the semillon or change to a dry riesling with the swordfish, and finish with a sweet, floral dessert wine and coffee.

al fresco evening grill for 6

rosemary and sea-salt grilled flatbreads
smoked eggplant and white bean puree
coriander prawns with honey bok choy
kaffir salmon with grilled limes
tequila, lime and ruby grapefruit sorbet

FOOD PREP
Start with the rosemary and sea-salt grilled flatbreads with the smoked eggplant (aubergine) and white bean puree. Make the puree and the flatbread dough ahead of time. Place the rolled flatbread dough in the freezer to stop the yeast over proving* the bread. Small servings of the coriander (cilantro) prawns (shrimp) with honey bok choy make good starters and then move on to the kaffir salmon with grilled limes (x 1½). Finish with the tequila, lime and ruby grapefruit sorbet, which can be made up to 2 days in advance. To serve the sorbet on a hot night, scoop it into chilled bowls and serve or, if you have room in the freezer, refreeze the sorbet in the serving bowls.

LIQUID SUGGESTIONS
A sparkling white is always a good way to start an evening outside. At the end of the day, some people may appreciate a good cold beer. Both the prawns (shrimp) and the salmon would be good with a chenin blanc or a sauvignon blanc. The sorbet can be served with a little extra tequila, or serve coffee and a liqueur after the sorbet.

SANDWICH BOX

portable food

basics

To ensure that your food reaches your destination in the best possible condition, you will need to put some thought into containers. If, for instance, you have baked frittatas in muffin tins, it is best to transport the frittatas in the tin, wrapping a clean towel around the tin and tying the ends in a knot for a handle. Ask your grandmother if she still has a cake tin with a tight-fitting lid. They're very handy!

picnic baskets

These can often be hard to carry when they are full and heavy. You may want to take a basket with two handles, so that the load is shared. Baskets are great for carrying glasses, plates and cutlery.

containers with lids

Be sure you have the right container for the job. Some container lids seal but are not watertight. This could be a disaster if you are carrying food with a dressing or sauce. To test whether your container is watertight, half fill it with water. Place the lid on your container and, over the sink, turn it upside down and sideways, and generally give it a good shake. If the water doesn't leak out, you know your food will be safe.

rugs and chairs

Take one more rug than you think will be necessary because you'll probably need it. Remove the contents from baskets and turn them upside down for a table for the food, or use the top of your chiller. A cushion is perfect picnic seating. Fold-up chairs can be bulky, heavy and hard to carry.

utensils

Depending on the type of portable event you are planning or attending, you may wish to take glassware, plates and other breakables. Be sure that you wrap them individually in the napkins you are taking with you. Place cutlery in cutlery rolls to keep everything together.

chillers

Also known as eskies, these are great if you are going out on a hot day. Fill them with ice or freezer blocks, and stack them with drinks, salads, meat and cheeses. If you want to cut down on baggage, a chiller is a good place to fit plates or serving ware. Glassware can be stacked in the chiller if you are using cubed ice.

flasks and hip flasks

Vacuum flasks are a great way to carry warm or cold drinks. Be sure to warm or cool the flask before pouring in the liquid. Hip flasks are small and discreet, handy for carrying a dash of something to add to the Champagne or fruit cordial.

containers

chiller

flasks

picnic box

chair and cushions

limeade + spiked passionfruit cordial

thai leaves and chicken baguettes & fresh corn cakes

limeade

1½ cups (12 fl oz) lime juice
¾ cup sugar
crushed ice
soda or mineral water
2 limes, sliced

Place the lime juice and sugar in a jug and stir until the sugar is dissolved. Refrigerate until cold. When ready to serve, place the lime mixture in an ice-filled glass and top with soda or mineral water and lime slices. Serves 6 to 8.

spiked passionfruit cordial

1½ cups (12 fl oz) orange juice, strained
1½ cups (12 fl oz) water
1 cup sugar
1 cup (8 fl oz) passionfruit pulp
½–¾ cup (4–6 fl oz) vodka or gin

Place the orange juice, water and sugar in a saucepan over medium heat and stir until the sugar is dissolved. Bring to the boil, simmer for 3 minutes then add the passionfruit pulp. Remove from the heat and allow to cool. Add the alcohol and store in sterilised bottles* in the fridge. Serve the cordial with soda water or Champagne. Serves 6 to 8.

antipasto picnic bread

1 large round loaf crusty bread
3 onions, sliced
2 tablespoons olive oil
12 slices char-grilled (broiled) marinated eggplant (aubergine)
½ cup mint leaves
20 slices char-grilled (broiled) marinated zucchini (courgette)
1 cup rocket (arugula) leaves
20 oven-roasted tomato halves
½ cup basil leaves
250g (8 oz) goat's cheese or fresh ricotta
20 slices char-grilled (broiled) capsicum (bell pepper) pieces

Cut the top from the bread and scoop out the soft insides leaving a 4cm (1½ in) thick crust. Place the onions and oil in a frying pan over medium heat and cook for 6 minutes or until well browned.
Place half the onions, eggplant, mint, zucchini, rocket, tomatoes, basil, cheese and capsicum inside the bread cavity in layers. Repeat the layers and replace the top of the bread. Wrap the loaf in a cloth to transport and cut into wedges to serve. Serves 8.

fresh corn cakes

3 cobs corn, husks and silk removed
550g (1 lb 4 oz) pumpkin, peeled and chopped
½ cup couscous
½ cup (4 fl oz) boiling water
¼ teaspoon ground cumin
1 red chilli, seeded and chopped
sea salt and cracked black pepper
flour to coat

Place the corn and pumpkin in a large saucepan of boiling water and cook for 5–8 minutes or until soft. Drain and mash the pumpkin. Remove the corn kernels from the cobs.
Place the couscous in a bowl and pour over the boiling water. Allow to stand for 5 minutes or until the couscous is tender. Combine the couscous, corn kernels, pumpkin, cumin, chilli, salt and pepper.
With wet hands, shape the mixture into small patties. Toss lightly in flour. To cook the patties, heat 2cm (¾ in) of oil in a frying pan over high heat. Add the patties and cook for 2 minutes each side or until golden and crisp. Serve warm or cold with a spicy chutney. Makes 25.

Thai chicken baguettes

2 tablespoons lemon juice
2 teaspoons sesame oil
2 red chillies, seeded and chopped
2 tablespoons soy sauce
2 chicken breast fillets, thickly sliced
⅓ cup Thai basil leaves
⅓ cup coriander (cilantro) leaves
⅓ cup mint leaves
12 garlic chives, halved
1 baguette, cut into 4

To make the filling, place the lemon juice, sesame oil, chillies and soy sauce in a bowl and mix to combine. Add the chicken and toss to coat. Allow to marinate for 30 minutes. Combine the basil, coriander, mint and chives. Place the herbs in each baguette piece.
Preheat a char grill (broiler), barbecue or frying pan over high heat. Remove the chicken from the marinade, place on the grill and cook for 2 minutes each side or until cooked through. Pile the chicken onto the herbs in the baguettes and wrap to serve. Serves 4.

antipasto picnic bread

little sweet potato and sage frittatas

eggplant and potato tarts

signature beef pies

blueberry fig tart

eggplant and potato tarts

315g (10½ oz) ready-prepared puff pastry
topping
2 eggplants (aubergines), sliced
1 tablespoon olive oil
1 tablespoon olive oil, extra
3 potatoes, peeled and thinly sliced
3 brown onions, sliced
2 tablespoons lemon thyme leaves
3 cloves garlic, sliced
sea salt and cracked black pepper

Preheat the oven to 200°C (400°F). Roll out the pastry on a lightly floured surface until 3mm (⅛ in) thick. Cut into six 12cm (4¾ in) circles and place on trays lined with non-stick baking paper.
To make the topping, brush the eggplant slices lightly with oil and cook in a preheated hot frying pan for 2 minutes each side or until golden. Remove the eggplant from the pan and set aside.
Heat the extra oil in the pan, add the potato slices and cook for 2 minutes each side or until golden. Remove from the pan. Place the onions and lemon thyme in the pan and cook over medium heat for 8–10 minutes or until the onions are golden and soft. Allow to cool.
Spread the onion mixture onto the pastry circles and top with the eggplant, potato, garlic, salt and pepper. Drizzle the tarts with a little olive oil and bake for 20–25 minutes or until the pastry is golden and the topping is cooked. Serves 6.

signature beef pies

500g (1 lb) ready-prepared puff pastry
1 egg, lightly beaten
filling
1 tablespoon oil
2 onions, chopped
500g (1 lb) diced chuck steak
1 cup (8 fl oz) beef stock*
⅓ cup (2¾ fl oz) red wine
2 tablespoons Worcestershire sauce
2 tablespoons tomato paste
2 tablespoons plain (all-purpose) flour
4 tablespoons water
sea salt and cracked pepper to taste

To make the filling, heat the oil in a saucepan over high heat. Add the onions and cook for 3 minutes or until soft. Add the steak and cook for 4 minutes or until sealed. Add the stock, wine, Worcestershire sauce and tomato paste. Reduce the heat and simmer, uncovered, for 50 minutes or until the meat is tender. Combine the flour and water to make a paste and stir into the meat mixture. Bring the mixture to the boil and stir for 1 minute. Season to taste with salt and pepper. Remove from the heat and allow to cool.
Preheat the oven to 200°C (400°F). Roll out the pastry on a lightly floured surface until 2mm (⅛ in) thick. Cut to fit the bases and sides of 6 small pie tins. Place the filling in the pastry bases and top with pastry circles. Press with a fork to seal.
From the pastry scraps, cut out names, letters or numbers and place on top of the pies. Brush the pie tops with the egg and bake the pies for 15–20 minutes or until the pastry is puffed and golden. Makes 6.

little sweet potato and sage frittatas

500g (1 lb) orange sweet potato (kumara), peeled and diced
olive oil
sea salt
4 eggs, lightly beaten
1 cup (8 fl oz) cream (single or pouring)
cracked black pepper
⅓ cup grated parmesan cheese
¼ cup small sage leaves

Preheat the oven to 200°C (400°F). Place the sweet potato, oil and salt in a baking dish and toss to combine. Bake for 25 minutes or until the sweet potato is soft.
Place the eggs, cream, pepper and parmesan in a bowl and whisk to combine. Pour into 12 greased shallow patty tins. Sprinkle with the sweet potato and sage leaves. Reduce the oven temperature to 160°C (315°F) and bake the frittatas for 20 minutes or until golden and firm to touch. Serve warm or cold with a spicy relish. Makes 12.

blueberry fig tart

1 quantity (350g or 12 oz) sweet shortcrust pastry*
8 fresh figs
125g (4 oz) blueberries
filling
175g (6 oz) butter, softened
1 cup caster (superfine) sugar
250g (8 oz) almond meal
4 eggs
¾ cup plain (all-purpose) flour
2 teaspoons finely grated lemon rind

Roll out the pastry on a lightly floured surface until 2mm (⅛ in) thick. Place in a deep 23cm (9 in) tart tin. Prick holes in the pastry base and refrigerate for 30 minutes. Preheat the oven to 200°C (400°F). Line the pastry with non-stick baking paper and fill with baking weights or rice. Bake for 5 minutes. Remove the weights or rice and paper, and bake for 5 minutes or until the pastry is a light golden colour.
To make the filling, place the butter and sugar in a bowl and beat until light and creamy. Add the almond meal, eggs, flour and lemon rind and mix until combined. Spread this mixture over the pastry. Cut 2 slits through the stems in the tops of the figs. Press the figs into the almond meal mixture in the tin and sprinkle with the blueberries. Reduce the oven temperature to 180°C (350°F) and bake the tart for 35 minutes or until the filling is firm and the figs are soft. Serve warm or cold with clotted cream. Serves 8 to 10.

coconut cake with mint syrup

125g (4 oz) butter
2 teaspoons grated lemon rind
1 cup caster (superfine) sugar
3 eggs
2 cups desiccated coconut
1 cup plain (all-purpose) flour
1 teaspoon baking powder
⅓ cup sour cream
mint syrup
1 cup sugar
2 tablespoons lemon juice
¾ cup (6 fl oz) water
½ cup mint leaves

Preheat the oven to 160°C (315°F). Place the butter, lemon rind and sugar in the bowl of an electric mixer and beat until light and creamy. Add the eggs, one at a time, and beat well. Fold through the coconut, flour and sour cream, and mix until combined.
Spoon the mixture into a 20cm (8 in) round cake tin lined with non-stick baking paper and bake for 45 minutes or until the cake is cooked when tested with a skewer.
To make the mint syrup, place the sugar, lemon juice, water and mint in a saucepan over low heat and stir until the sugar is dissolved. Allow the syrup to simmer for 3 minutes, then strain. Pour the hot syrup over the hot cake. Keep the cake in a tin and cover with a lid to transport. Serve in wedges with clotted cream. Serves 8 to 10.

double choc brownies

240g (7½ oz) butter
240g (7½ oz) dark chocolate
3 eggs
1½ cups caster (superfine) sugar
2 cups plain (all-purpose) flour
½ teaspoon baking powder
1½ cups roughly chopped white chocolate

Preheat the oven to 180°C (350°F). Place the butter and dark chocolate in a saucepan over very low heat and stir until smooth. Set aside.
Place the eggs and caster sugar in a bowl and beat until light and thick. Fold the egg mixture through the chocolate mixture. Add the flour, baking powder and white chocolate and fold through. Pour into a greased 23cm (9 in) square cake tin lined with non-stick baking paper. Bake for 40 minutes or until set.
Allow to cool, cut into squares and dust with icing (confectioner's) sugar or good-quality cocoa powder. Makes 24 squares.

coconut cake with mint syrup

double choc brownies

menu ideas

picnic at the polo for 8

fresh corn cakes
little sweet potato and sage frittatas
eggplant and potato tarts
blueberry fig tart
spiked passionfruit cordial

FOOD PREP
Start with the fresh corn cakes and a spicy chutney, and the little sweet potato and sage frittatas. Serve the eggplant (aubergine) and potato tarts (x 1½) for mains with a salad of mixed green leaves dressed with balsamic vinegar and olive oil. The blueberry fig tart makes a wonderful late-afternoon dessert with coffee and tea. Prepare the recipes the day before, and do the cooking the morning of the picnic.

LIQUID SUGGESTIONS
Start the day with a crisp, sparkling white wine and some spiked passionfruit cordial. Move on to a grassy sauvignon blanc with the nibbles and a lightly wooded chardonnay with the tarts. If the afternoon gets chilly, dispense a little cognac or brandy from a hip flask to accompany the blueberry fig tart.

picnic by the lake for 6

little sweet potato and sage frittatas
antipasto picnic bread
double choc brownies
limeade

FOOD PREP
Try a wrapped box of little sweet potato and sage frittatas for starters followed by the king of the picnic, the antipasto picnic bread, cut into chunky wedges and served with limeade. Prepare the recipes the day before, and do the cooking and baking the morning of the picnic. Finish with sweet, rich double choc brownies, which can be made 2 days in advance and stored in an airtight container.

LIQUID SUGGESTIONS
Take a chiller (esky) full of ice and place it in the shade under a tree. Fill it with limeade and sparkling mineral water, a lightly wooded chardonnay and a bottle of smooth merlot to sip the afternoon away. Have a thermos of hot coffee to serve with the brownies.

picnic at the races for 8

eggplant and potato tarts
Thai chicken baguettes
coconut cake with mint syrup

FOOD PREP
Cut the eggplant and potato tarts into small pieces to nibble with drinks. Serve the Thai chicken baguettes (double the recipe) wrapped in napkins for lunch, and later in the afternoon serve the coconut cake with mint syrup, which can be made a day in advance and stored in an airtight container. Prepare the other recipes the day before, and do the cooking and baking the morning of the picnic.

LIQUID SUGGESTIONS
When you think races, you think bubbly whites and celebrations. You may choose to drink sparkling white all day long. The spicy baguettes would also be great with a dry riesling. All those bubbles can make a person a little weary, so a short black with some sweet coconut cake will liven everyone up again for the journey home.

drinks

basics

For a successful drinks party, make sure you have all the bar accessories and drink-making supplies in order before the guests arrive. When serving tricky morsels, be sure your guests have a place to put their prawn tails and scallop shells. Otherwise, you'll be finding abandoned debris in your pot plants for months to come.

ice

You can never have too much ice at a drinks party. Fill large buckets with cubed ice to chill champagne, wine and mixers at least 1 hour before guests arrive. Have plenty of ice at the bar for cocktails. Set a block of ice on a tray with an icepick for large, cooling shards of ice for drinks.

corkscrew

The old-fashioned and extremely reliable waiter's friend corkscrew is a must. Plain stainless steel will serve you well for years. If you are planning to have many guests, make sure you have a few corkscrews. If you misplace your only one, there will be no party!

blender

If you want to make drinks with lots of crushed ice, make sure you have a blender with a little power behind it. You won't necessarily need a commercial blender, but a glass jug and good 400-watt-or-above motor will do the job well.

cocktail shaker

Almost every home bar seems to have a cocktail shaker on a shelf collecting dust. What you may have thought was a token bar element is an essential item. Be aware that cocktail shakers range in price.

ice crusher

If you are going to serve drinks over crushed ice, you may need to invest in an ice crusher. Manual ones are fairly inexpensive, or you can go for the fully electrified version. Or wrap the ice in a tea towel and smash against a hard surface.

glasses

Make sure you have plenty of glasses and hire extras if you need to. Glasses don't have to strictly match the cocktail, but a small range is good: large glasses for icy fruit daiquiris and frozen margaritas, and smaller glasses for the more potent berry martini.

swizzle sticks and bits

Search for fun swizzle sticks, straws and drink accessories. Don't be restrained by good taste or a subtle colour scheme— the more pink flamingoes and fake fruit, the better.

ice crusher

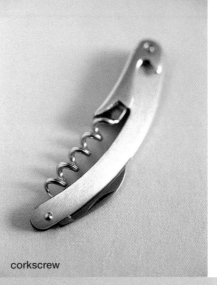

corkscrew

cocktail shaker

blender

straws and swizzle sticks

lime and ginger scallops

vanilla vodka

lime and ginger scallops

24 scallops in half shell
lime and ginger butter
2 tablespoons very finely shredded ginger
2 teaspoons finely grated lime rind
2 teaspoons sesame oil
cracked black pepper
2 tablespoons lemon thyme leaves
100g (3½ oz) butter, softened slightly

To make the lime and ginger butter, place the ginger, lime rind, sesame oil, pepper, thyme and butter in a bowl and mix to combine. Spread a little of the seasoned butter over each scallop. Before serving, place the scallops under a preheated very hot grill (broiler) and cook for 1 minute or until golden. Be careful not to overcook the scallops as the shell heats up and continues cooking them. Serve immediately. Makes 24.

vanilla vodka

750ml (24 fl oz) vodka
3 vanilla beans,* split

Place the vanilla beans in the vodka and allow to infuse on a windowsill for at least 1 week. To serve straight, freeze the vodka with the vanilla beans for 24 hours prior to serving. Serve the vanilla vodka over ice with tonic or soda. Makes 750ml (24 fl oz).

Campari and ruby grapefruit

500ml (16 fl oz) bottled ruby grapefruit juice
⅓ cup (2¾ fl oz) Campari
6 mint sprigs
315ml (10 fl oz) tonic or soda water
ice

Place the grapefruit juice, Campari, mint and tonic or soda in a jug and stir to combine. Pour into chilled glasses filled with ice and serve. Serves 3 to 4.

iced berry martini

½ cup (4 fl oz) gin
⅓ cup (2¾ fl oz) sweet vermouth
8 ice cubes
4 tablespoons pureed berries

Place the gin, vermouth, ice and berry puree in a cocktail shaker. Shake well and strain into well-chilled glasses. Serves 2.

seared and marinated tuna

500g (1 lb) piece sashimi tuna
2 teaspoons sesame oil
2 teaspoons ginger, minced
4 tablespoons soy sauce
2 tablespoons mirin (see page 32)
2 tablespoons lemon juice
1 tablespoon finely chopped flat-leaf parsley
1 quantity sushi rice*
3 sheets toasted nori*
pickled ginger■

Brush the tuna with the sesame oil. Heat a frying pan over high heat, add the tuna and cook for 5 seconds each side. Set aside.
Combine the ginger, soy sauce, mirin, lemon juice and parsley in a shallow dish. Place the tuna in the marinade and refrigerate, turning the tuna occasionally, for 1–2 hours. To serve, remove the tuna from the marinade and slice thinly. Place half of the rice on a piece of non-stick baking paper and place the paper on a sushi rolling mat (see page 32). Roll the rice in the paper and mat until a firm cylinder. With a serrated knife, cut the rice into discs 2cm (¾ in) thick. Repeat with the remaining rice. Cut the nori into squares bigger than the rice discs and place the squares on a serving platter.
To serve, top each nori square with a rice disc, a piece of pickled ginger and a slice of tuna. Spoon over a little of the marinade and serve. Makes 32 pieces.
■ Available from Asian food stores.

Pimm's citrus crush

⅓ cup (2¾ fl oz) freshly crushed lemon juice
⅓ cup (2¾ fl oz) freshly crushed lime juice
⅓ cup (2¾ fl oz) freshly crushed orange juice
⅓ cup (2¾ fl oz) freshly crushed ruby grapefruit juice
1 tablespoon caster (superfine) sugar
500ml (16 fl oz) tonic water
½ cup (4 fl oz) Pimm's no. 1

Place the lemon, lime, orange and ruby grapefruit juices in a jug. Add the sugar and stir to dissolve. Add the tonic and Pimm's, and serve over ice. Serves 4 to 6.

classic Champagne framboise

750ml (24 fl oz) bottle Champagne or sparkling white wine
10 tablespoons framboise* or raspberry liqueur
fresh raspberries

Place the Champagne on ice 1 hour before serving. Divide the framboise between 4 glasses. Top with Champagne and raspberries. Serves 4.

seared and marinated tuna

iced berry martini + classic Champagne framboise

Campari and ruby grapefruit + Pimm's citrus crush

balsamic fig bruschetta

frozen vodka slushie

white lime

balsamic fig bruschetta

1 tablespoon butter

1/4 cup (2 fl oz) balsamic vinegar

2 teaspoons sugar

6 figs, cut into quarters

filling

250g (8 oz) blue cheese (with bite and body)

1/3 cup (135g or 4 1/2 oz) mascarpone*

1 tablespoon roughly chopped flat-leaf parsley

cracked black pepper

bruschetta

24 thin slices sourdough baguette

olive oil

3 cloves garlic, halved

To make the filling, combine the blue cheese, mascarpone, parsley and pepper to taste.

To prepare the figs, heat the butter, balsamic vinegar and sugar in a frying pan over high heat. Stir and allow to simmer until the mixture thickens slightly. Place the fig quarters in the pan, a few at a time, and cook for 30 seconds each side or until lightly coated. Set aside. To make the bruschetta, brush the baguette slices with the oil. Place under a hot grill (broiler) and cook until the bread is golden on both sides. When cooked, rub the bread with the garlic halves.

To serve, place a small amount of the blue cheese mixture on each slice of bread and top with a fig. Warm the bruschetta under a low grill before serving. Makes 24.

salmon and pickled cucumber

300g (10 oz) piece sashimi salmon

24 triangles of Lebanese bread or flatbread

pickled cucumbers

2 Lebanese cucumbers, thinly sliced

sea salt

1/4 cup (2 fl oz) white wine vinegar

1 tablespoon chopped dill

2 teaspoons caster (superfine) sugar

1–2 teaspoons wasabi*

cracked black pepper

To make the pickled cucumbers, place the cucumber slices in a colander and sprinkle with sea salt. Allow the cucumbers to drain for 15 minutes. Wash and pat dry the slices with paper towel and place in a bowl. Combine the vinegar, dill, sugar, wasabi and pepper. Pour over the cucumbers and allow to marinate for 30 minutes.

To serve, cut the salmon into 24 slices. Place a piece of salmon to one side of the bread. Drain cucumbers and place a small pile of cucumber slices on top of the salmon. Make a slit in the side of each bread triangle and thread the corner through the opposite corner, or secure with a toothpick and serve. Makes 24 pieces.

frozen vodka slushie

1 cup sugar

4 cups (32 fl oz) boiling water

1 1/2 cups (12 fl oz) lemon or lime juice

1/2 –3/4 cup (4–6 fl oz) vodka

Place the sugar and boiling water in a bowl and stir until the sugar is dissolved. Allow the mixture to cool slightly before adding the lemon or lime juice and vodka. Place the mixture in the freezer and leave for 2 hours. Stir with a fork and freeze for another 2 hours or until firm. Break the ice with a fork or blend until smooth and serve immediately. Serves 4.

white lime

750ml (24 fl oz) white spirit, such as vodka, gin or white rum

4 limes, sliced

Place the spirit and limes in a clean bottle and refrigerate. Allow the limes to infuse into the spirit for at least 4 days before serving over ice, with soda or tonic. To serve straight, place the limes and spirit in the freezer for a few hours. Makes 750ml (24 fl oz).

kaffir chicken on betel leaves

2 teaspoons sesame oil

1 tablespoon finely shredded ginger

1 stalk lemongrass,* finely chopped

6 kaffir lime* leaves, shredded

3 red chillies, seeded and chopped

300g (10 oz) minced chicken breast

2 tablespoons lemon juice

1 tablespoon fish sauce

2 tablespoons soy sauce

12–18 betel leaves* or baby English spinach leaves to serve

coriander (cilantro) sprigs and sliced chilli to serve

Place the sesame oil in a frying pan or wok over high heat. Add the ginger, lemongrass, lime leaves and chillies and cook for 1 minute. Add the chicken and cook for 4 minutes or until cooked. Stir through the lemon juice, fish sauce and soy sauce, and cook for 1 minute. Wash the betel or spinach leaves and dry on paper towel. Place piles of the warm chicken filling on each leaf and serve immediately with a sprig of coriander and some sliced chilli. Makes 12 to 18 pieces.

kaffir chicken on betel leaves

sesame and soy pumpkin

750g (1½ lb) sweet pumpkin
oil
sea salt
3 tablespoons honey
2 teaspoons sesame oil
1 tablespoon sesame seeds
1 tablespoon finely chopped ginger
3 tablespoons soy sauce
2 tablespoons Chinese cooking (shao hsing) wine
  (see page 32) or sherry

Preheat the oven to 200°C (400°F). Peel the pumpkin, cut into bite-sized pieces and toss in oil and salt. Place in a single layer in a baking dish and bake for 25 minutes or until tender.
Combine the honey, sesame oil, sesame seeds, ginger, soy sauce and wine. Place in a large frying pan over medium heat and allow to simmer until quite syrupy. Add the pumpkin, a few pieces at a time, and toss to coat. Remove the pumpkin from the pan and place on a baking tray lined with non-stick baking paper. Reduce the oven temperature to 150°C (300°F) and bake the pumpkin again. Serve warm with toothpicks. Makes 24 pieces.

chilli and lemon olives

500g (1 lb) firm kalamata olives
3 cloves garlic, unpeeled
2 red chillies, chopped
3 tablespoons lemon juice
1 tablespoon shredded lemon rind
1 tablespoon rosemary leaves
3 tablespoons olive oil

Before marinating the olives, test them for saltiness. If the olives are salty, place them in a large bowl of cold water. Drain the olives and place them in fresh water every 30 minutes until they are no longer overly salty.
Place the garlic in a dry frying pan over high heat and toast on all sides until well browned. Remove the garlic from its skin and mash. Combine with the chillies, lemon juice and rind, rosemary and oil. Pour the marinade over the olives and refrigerate for at least 8 hours (2–3 days is best) before serving. Serves 6 to 8.

duck liver pâté

550g (1 lb 1¾ oz) duck livers
½ cup (4 fl oz) cognac
2 tablespoons butter
1 teaspoon tarragon leaves
¼ teaspoon grated nutmeg
cracked black pepper
75g (2½ oz) butter, extra, chopped

Remove any discoloured or tough white pieces of liver. Place the livers in a bowl with the cognac and refrigerate for 2 hours. Heat the butter in a large frying pan over high heat until bubbling. Drain the livers, reserving the cognac, and add the livers to the pan. Tossthe livers in the butter until they change colour. Remove from the pan. Add the cognac, tarragon, nutmeg and pepper to the pan and cook for 2–3 minutes or until the liquid is reduced to a third. Process the livers and the cognac mixture in a food processor until smooth. Press the liver mixture through a fine sieve and return to the cleaned food processor. Add the extra butter to the liver mixture and process until smooth. Transfer to a bowl, cover with plastic wrap and refrigerate for 2–3 hours or until firm. Serve the pâté on toasted slices of bagel with pepper pears. Serves 12.

pepper pears

3 tablespoons apple cider vinegar
2 tablespoons balsamic vinegar
2 tablespoons sugar
cracked black pepper
2 firm pears, peeled and thinly sliced

Place the cider vinegar, balsamic vinegar, sugar and pepper in a frying pan over low heat and stir until the sugar is dissolved. Add the pears and allow to simmer for 1 minute. Remove the pan from the heat and allow the pears to stand for 1 hour before serving at room temperature with the pâté. Serves 12.

peach julep

1 cup (8 fl oz) water
½ cup sugar
1½ cups mint leaves
1½ cups (12 fl oz) fresh white peach juice, chilled
½–¾ cup (4–6 fl oz) bourbon or brandy
soda

Place the water and sugar in a saucepan over low heat and stir until the sugar is dissolved. Add the mint leaves and simmer for 3 minutes. Remove from the heat and allow to stand for 30 minutes. Strain the syrup, add to the peach juice and bourbon, and mix to combine. Refrigerate.

sesame and soy pumpkin

chilli and lemon olives

salmon and pickled cucumber

duck liver pâté with pepper pears

113

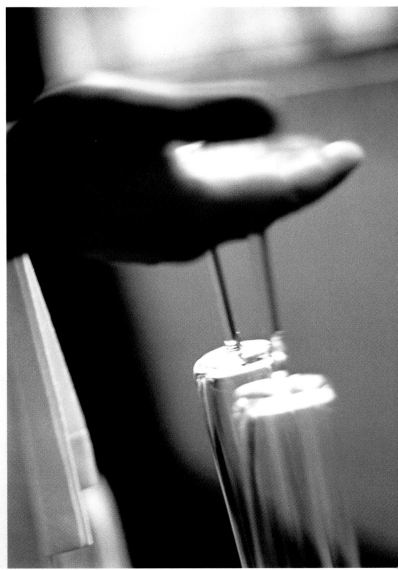

peach julep

menu ideas

pre-dinner drinks for 8

balsamic fig bruschetta
sesame and soy pumpkin
lime and ginger scallops
Pimm's citrus crush
classic Champagne framboise

FOOD PREP
As a prelude to dining and to awaken the tastebuds, start with the balsamic fig bruschetta, followed by the sesame and soy pumpkin, and the lime and ginger grilled scallops. If there is enough food with the drinks, you can go straight into mains for dinner followed by dessert and cheese. The balsamic fig bruschetta and the pumpkin can be made ahead of time and gently warmed before serving. Prepare the lime and ginger butter for the scallops beforehand and grill (broil) the scallops just before serving.

LIQUID SUGGESTIONS
Start with something light and refreshing such as the Pimm's citrus crush or the classic Champagne framboise. Serve a rich pinot noir, a mellow cabernet sauvignon or an aged chardonnay to complement the food.

celebration drinks party for 10

lime and ginger scallops
chilli and lemon olives
duck liver pâté
pepper pears
balsamic fig bruschetta
classic Champagne framboise

FOOD PREP
When your guests arrive, serve the lime and ginger scallops. Follow these with small cups or beakers of the chilli and lemon olives served with small olive forks. The duck liver pâté with pepper pears and the balsamic fig bruschetta will make a substantial finish. You can make the pâté and pears prior to the party and marinate the olives the day before.

LIQUID SUGGESTIONS
When your guests arrive, serve a classic Champagne framboise (double the quantities), straight bubbly or a light pinot noir. To carry them through the evening, keep serving the bubbly and maybe add a smooth cabernet sauvignon to complement the rich pâté and bruschetta.

cocktails for 6

sesame and soy pumpkin
seared and marinated tuna
kaffir chicken on betel leaves
frozen vodka slushie
Campari and ruby grapefruit
vanilla vodka

FOOD PREP
Start with the sesame and soy pumpkin, and the seared and marinated tuna. After these, the kaffir chicken on betel leaves will fill stomachs nicely. All recipes can be prepared beforehand. Warm the pumpkin and the chicken topping for the leaves before serving.

LIQUID SUGGESTIONS
Start off strong with frozen vodka slushies (triple the quantities), moving on to Campari and ruby grapefruit. A good, well-flavoured cold beer is also great if it is a hot summer night, so fill a large tub with ice. Serve the vanilla vodka over ready-made fruit sorbet to finish.

in a flash

basics

oils and vinegars

A splash of oil or vinegar can become the flavour saviour of a quickly put-together meal. Be sure to buy oils and vinegars of good quality. Like many things, you pay for what you get. Store them in a cool, dark place.

OLIVE OIL Have a light olive oil as well as a good, deep green, fruity, extra-virgin one on hand for varying intensities of flavour.

SESAME OIL Buy a good-quality Asian sesame oil and use it sparingly as it may overpower other flavours.

CHILLI OIL The strength of the heat varies from extreme to mild, so test before splashing chilli oil* into a dish. It is a great way to add chilli flavour in a hurry.

VEGETABLE OIL This oil is good for frying and when you wish to use a mild oil in dressings.

HERB OILS These are great in dressings or as a base for a well-flavoured dish.

WHITE WINE AND RED WINE VINEGAR Purchase good-quality wine vinegars for the best flavours.

BALSAMIC VINEGAR Balsamic vinegar is aged in a similar way to wine and, like wine, good quality is a must.

HERB VINEGAR These vinegars are a great base for a fast salad dressing. It's easy to make your own.

sauces, pastes and preserves

For great flavour bases for quick and tasty marinades, dressings or additions to salads or pastas, keep a good selection of sauces and condiments in the cupboard. Check their labels, as some need to be refrigerated after opening.

SOY SAUCE, OYSTER SAUCE, CHILLI SAUCE, FISH SAUCE Keep a variety of these sauces handy for marinades, dipping sauces, curries, stir-fries and much more (see page 32).

CRACKED BLACK PEPPER AND SEA SALT Use peppercorns in a grinder for freshly cracked pepper. When using sea salt, grind the rock form or crush the flaked variety in your fingertips before adding to food.

DRIED CHILLIES, SEEDS AND HERBS Buy these in small amounts as their flavour will fade. Store dried chillies, seeds and herbs in airtight containers. Grind whole spices as required.

WASABI This is an addictive green horseradish paste. It's a must-have for sushi or marinades. You can buy wasabi* in paste or powdered form. (I prefer the Japanese paste form.)

MUSTARDS AND CHUTNEYS These can save a sandwich, a marinade, a dressing and much more. Keep a good variety at close range. I keep onion marmalade; seeded, Dijon and honey mustards; chilli jam; mango and lemongrass chutneys; and whatever else I can find with a bit of spice or kick.

OLIVES AND CAPERS Keep these in jars in the cupboard or fridge. They are great to add to salads, sandwiches and pastas for a little saltiness and zing.

store cupboard essentials

Keep a good selection of dry goods in your store cupboard so you have the basic building blocks to create a great meal at short notice.

LONG-LIFE STOCK PACKS The quality of these varies, so test them out. In a perfect world we would have time to make our own stock. Good-quality frozen stock is available at some stores.

DRIED PASTA AND NOODLES These solve many a 'nothing for dinner' dilemma. Keep a good variety in the cupboard as standbys.

JASMINE RICE, RISOTTO RICE AND SHORT-GRAIN RICE These are essential accompaniments for quick stir-fries or curries. My favourite, arborio*, takes a little longer to prepare, but it's therapeutic to sit on a stool sipping a glass of wine while stirring risotto.

POLENTA It's extremely rewarding on a chilly night to sit down to some soft polenta with fried herbs, blue cheese and pepper.

LENTILS From red to green to brown, lentils make a great base for salads, soups and curries.

COUSCOUS Cover couscous with boiling stock, toss through a little butter, pepper and herbs, and hey presto. Eat it hot with meat or vegetables, or cold in a salad.

COOKING WINES A dry red and a dry white wine, and a bottle of mirin (see page 32) will fit the bill. Don't buy really cheap wine as the flavour will come through in your cooking.

balsamic vinegar

herb oil and chilli oil

vegetable oil, olive oil and sesame oil

red and white wine vinegars

herb vinegar

mustards and chutneys   dried spices and chillies

salt and pepper   preserved goods

pastes

red and white cooking wines

pasta and noodles

STOCK

stock

rice

lentils and grains

roast fennel and olive salad

rocket and parmesan flatbread salad

roast fennel and olive salad

4 baby fennel bulbs, quartered
2 red onions, cut into eight pieces
4 roma tomatoes,* halved
3 tablespoons olive oil
2 tablespoons oregano leaves
beet leaves or salad greens
1 cup Ligurian or small olives
dressing
3 tablespoons apple cider vinegar
2 teaspoons Dijon mustard
2 tablespoons olive oil
1 clove garlic, crushed

Preheat the oven to 200°C (400°F). Place the fennel, onions and tomatoes in a baking dish. Heat the oil in a small saucepan over low heat. Add the oregano and heat for 3 minutes. Pour the oil over the vegetables and bake for 30 minutes. To make the dressing, whisk together the vinegar, mustard, oil and garlic. To serve, place the vegetables on a bed of beet or salad greens on serving plates. Sprinkle with the olives and dressing. Serves 4 as a starter, or serve with grilled meats or fish as a main meal.

mint couscous with fried tomatoes

1½ cups couscous
1¾ cups (14 fl oz) boiling vegetable* or chicken stock*
1 tablespoon olive oil
4 ripe tomatoes, thickly sliced
cracked black pepper
2 teaspoons oil, extra
1 onion, chopped
2 tablespoons salted baby capers, rinsed and dried
1 tablespoon grated lemon rind
¼ cup roughly chopped blanched almonds
3 tablespoons chopped mint
100g (3½ oz) rocket (arugula) leaves
175g (6 oz) marinated feta cheese, sliced

Place the couscous in a bowl and pour over the boiling stock. Allow to stand for 5 minutes or until the stock has been absorbed. Heat the oil in a large frying pan over medium heat. Sprinkle the tomato slices with pepper and add to the pan. Cook for 4–5 minutes each side or until well browned. Heat the extra oil in a separate frying pan over high heat. Add the onion and cook for 3 minutes or until soft. Add the capers, lemon rind and almonds and cook for 2 minutes. Add the couscous and mint and cook for 2 minutes or until heated through. Place the couscous on plates, top with the rocket, cheese and fried tomatoes. Serves 6 as a starter or 4 as a main meal.

rocket and parmesan flatbread salad

2 bunches (200g or 7 oz) rocket (arugula) leaves
3 tablespoons balsamic vinegar
2 ruby grapefruit, peeled and segmented
½–¾ cup shaved parmesan cheese
cracked black pepper
parmesan flatbread
2 flat lavash breads
⅓ cup finely grated parmesan cheese
¼ cup (2 fl oz) olive oil

Combine the rocket, balsamic vinegar, grapefruit, parmesan and pepper in a bowl.
To make the parmesan flatbread, cut the lavash into 16 equal pieces. Combine the parmesan and oil, and brush over one side of the bread strips. Place under a preheated hot grill (broiler) and cook for 1 minute or until golden. Turn the bread, brush with the parmesan mixture and grill for 1 minute or until golden.
Cross 4 bread strips on each plate. Top with the rocket and serve. Serves 4 as a starter or as a salad with a char-grilled (broiled) meat or fish main meal.

noodle bowl with barbecue pork

8 dried Chinese mushrooms
400g (13 oz) fresh udon* or Hokkien noodles
3 cups (24 fl oz) chicken stock*
½ cup (4 fl oz) Chinese cooking (shao hsing) wine (see page 32) or sherry
6 slices ginger
1 green chilli, seeded and sliced
4 green onions (scallions), chopped
2 tablespoons coriander (cilantro) leaves
2 cups chopped bok choy or choy sum (see page 32)
350g (12 oz) Chinese barbecue pork*

Place the mushrooms in a bowl, cover with boiling water and soak for 5 minutes or until soft. Drain, pat dry and finely slice.
Place the noodles in hot water for 1 minute, then drain. If you are using dried noodles, place in a saucepan of boiling water until soft, then drain. Divide the noodles among serving bowls.
Place the stock, wine, ginger, chilli, onions and coriander in a saucepan over high heat and bring to the boil. Add the greens then pour the stock over the noodles in the bowls. Slice the pork, place in the bowls with the noodles and toss to combine. Sprinkle with mushrooms before serving. Serve with chilli sauce or chopped chillies. Serves 6 as a starter or 4 as a main meal.

noodle bowl with barbecue pork

sesame-crusted ocean trout

4 x 180g (6 oz) pieces ocean trout fillet
1/4 cup sesame seeds
1/4 cup black sesame seeds*
1 tablespoon oil
greens
1 bunch gai larn (see page 32), trimmed and halved
1 bunch choy sum (see page 32), trimmed and halved
2 teaspoons sesame oil
1 tablespoon shredded ginger
3 tablespoons oyster sauce
2 tablespoons soy sauce
1 tablespoon sugar
3 tablespoons Chinese cooking (shao hsing) wine
  (see page 32) or sherry

Remove the skin and visible bones from the trout. Combine the white and black sesame seeds and place them in a shallow dish. Press both sides of the trout pieces into the sesame seeds to form a crust.

Place the greens in a saucepan of boiling water and cook for 1 minute, then drain.

Heat the sesame oil in a saucepan over high heat. Add the ginger and cook for 1 minute. Add the oyster and soy sauces, sugar and wine, and simmer for 4 minutes or until thickened.

Place a frying pan over low heat. Add the oil and place the trout in the pan. Cook for 1–2 minutes each side or until cooked medium-rare. To serve, toss the greens in the frying pan with the simmering sauce and place on plates. Top the greens with the sesame-crusted trout. Serves 4.

lamb with garlic mash

8 double lamb cutlets, trimmed
1 teaspoon cracked black pepper
3 tablespoons chopped mint
1/2 cup (4 fl oz) red wine
1 tablespoon seeded mustard
1/4 teaspoon ground cumin
garlic mash
6 cloves garlic, unpeeled
6 mashing potatoes, peeled and chopped
2 tablespoons butter
1–1 1/4 cups (8–10 fl oz) hot milk
pinch sea salt

Place the lamb cutlets in a shallow dish. Combine the pepper, mint, wine, mustard and cumin. Pour over the lamb and allow to marinate for at least 30 minutes, preferably 2 hours.

To make the garlic mash, place the unpeeled garlic in a dry frying pan over medium heat. Allow to cook, turning occasionally, for 10 minutes or until the garlic skins are golden brown. Allow to cool. Squeeze the garlic from their skins and mash with a fork.

Place the potatoes in a saucepan of boiling water and simmer for 6 minutes or until tender. While the potatoes are cooking, drain the marinade from the lamb and place in a small saucepan. Allow the marinade to simmer over low heat until syrupy.

Heat a frying pan over high heat. Add the lamb and cook for 2–3 minutes each side or until cooked to your liking.

To finish the mash, drain the potatoes, return them to the warm pan with the butter, and mash with a whisk while slowly adding the milk until thick and creamy. Stir through the salt and mashed garlic.

To serve, place a pile of mash on plates with the lamb and spoon over the sauce. Serve with a salad of rocket (arugula) and balsamic vinegar, or baby spinach leaves. Serves 4.

jasmine rice pilaf with salt-roasted chicken

4 chicken breast fillets, skin on
olive oil
sea salt
jasmine rice pilaf
1 tablespoon oil
1 tablespoon butter
2 onions, chopped
2 coriander (cilantro) roots
4 kaffir lime* leaves
2 red chillies, seeded and chopped
1 1/2 cups jasmine rice
1 1/2 cups (12 fl oz) vegetable* or chicken stock*
1–1 1/2 cups (8–12 fl oz) water

Preheat the oven to 150°C (300°F). To cook the chicken, rub its skin with the oil and salt, being careful not to salt the flesh. Place a frying pan over high heat, add the chicken, skin-side down, and cook for 2 minutes or until well browned. Place the chicken in a baking dish and bake for 30 minutes.

To make the pilaf, heat the oil and butter in a heavy-based saucepan over medium heat. Add the onions and cook for 3 minutes or until soft. Add the coriander roots, kaffir lime leaves and chillies, and cook for 1 minute.

Add the rice and cook for 2 minutes. Add the stock and most of the water, then cover the pan and simmer over medium-low heat for 15 minutes or until the rice is soft and the liquid has been absorbed. More water may be added if required. Remove the lime leaves and coriander roots.

To serve, place the pilaf in bowls on the side of plates and place the chicken on the plates. Tomato pickle or spicy mango chutney make a good accompaniment. Serves 4.

mint couscous with fried tomatoes

sesame-crusted ocean trout

lamb with garlic mash   jasmine rice pilaf with salt-roasted chicken

linguine with asparagus and baked ricotta   ginger pork with lentils

spaghetti with lemon, chilli, garlic and rocket

400g (13 oz) dried spaghetti, linguine or fettuccine
3–4 tablespoons light olive oil
2 cloves garlic, crushed
4 tablespoons salted baby capers, rinsed
1½ teaspoons dried chilli flakes or 3 fresh red chillies,
    seeded and sliced
2 teaspoons finely grated lemon rind
3 tablespoons lemon juice
3–4 cups roughly chopped rocket (arugula)
¾ cup grated parmesan cheese
cracked black pepper

Place the spaghetti in a saucepan of rapidly boiling water
and cook until al dente.
While the pasta is cooking, heat the oil in a large saucepan
over high heat. Add the garlic and capers and cook for
1 minute. Add the chillies and lemon rind and juice, and
cook for another minute. Drain the pasta and add to the
garlic mixture with rocket and parmesan. Toss to combine
and serve with a generous sprinkling of pepper and warm,
crusty bread. Serves 6 as a starter or 4 (with salad) as a
main meal.

linguine with asparagus and baked ricotta

400g (13 oz) dried linguine
2 tablespoons butter
2 tablespoons oil
¾ cup chopped hazelnuts
3 tablespoons sage leaves
2 cloves garlic, crushed
3 tablespoons lemon juice
sea salt and cracked black pepper
3 bunches (600g or 1¼ lb) asparagus, trimmed and blanched
150g (5 oz) baby English spinach leaves
300g (10 oz) baked ricotta, sliced
balsamic vinegar

Place the linguine in a saucepan of boiling water and cook
for 10–12 minutes or until al dente.
While the pasta is cooking, heat the butter and oil in a frying
pan over high heat. Add the hazelnuts and sage, and cook
for 2–3 minutes or until the nuts are golden. Add the garlic
and cook for 1 minute. Add the lemon juice, salt, pepper,
asparagus and drained linguine and toss to combine.
To serve, place the spinach leaves on plates and top with
slices of ricotta. Place the linguine on the leaves and ricotta
and drizzle with balsamic vinegar. Serves 6 a starter or 4 as
a main meal.

ginger pork with lentils

1 tablespoon oil
2 tablespoons shredded ginger
1 tablespoon brown sugar
2 tablespoons lime juice
1 tablespoon balsamic vinegar
750g (1½ lb) pork fillet medallions 3cm (1¼ in) thick
refried lentils
1½ cups puy lentils▪
2½ cups (20 fl oz) water
1 tablespoon oil
2 teaspoons cumin seeds
1 tablespoon lime juice
2 tablespoons chopped coriander (cilantro)
sea salt and cracked black pepper

Heat the oil in a frying pan over high heat. Add the ginger
and cook for 2 minutes or until a light golden colour. Add
the sugar, lime juice and vinegar, and simmer until the
mixture thickens. Set aside.
To make the refried lentils, place the lentils and water in a
saucepan and bring to the boil. Reduce the heat, cover the
lentils and cook at a simmer for 5–8 minutes or until all the
liquid has been absorbed and the lentils have softened.
Heat the oil in a frying pan over high heat. Add the cumin
seeds and cook for 1 minute. Add the lentils, lime juice,
coriander, salt and pepper, and cook, stirring, for 5 minutes
or until the lentils are soft and heated through.
To cook the pork, heat a frying pan over high heat. Add the
pork medallions and cook for 2–3 minutes on each side or
until cooked to your liking. Pour over the caramelised ginger
and heat for 1 minute.
To serve, place the lentils on a plate and top with the pork
and ginger syrup. Serves 4.
▪ Small, dark and firm lentils available from delicatessens
and speciality food stores.

spaghetti with lemon, chilli, garlic and rocket

tamarillos soaked in sauternes

6 tamarillos (tree tomatoes)
1 cup (8 fl oz) water
1/2 cup sugar
1 vanilla bean,* halved
250ml (8 fl oz) sauternes or late-harvest riesling

Place the tamarillos in a saucepan of boiling water and cook for 1 minute. Drain and peel away the skins. Slice the tamarillos down the middle, leaving the stalk end intact. Place the water, sugar and vanilla bean in a saucepan over low heat and stir until the sugar is dissolved. Bring the syrup to the boil and simmer for 3 minutes. Add the tamarillos and sauternes, and remove the pan from the heat. Allow to stand for at least 1 hour or overnight. Serve the tamarillos in deep bowls with thick cream on the side. Serves 6.

autumn plum and strawberry crumbles

3 cups chopped ripe autumn plums
1 cup halved and hulled strawberries
2–3 tablespoons sugar
1/2 teaspoon ground cinnamon
2 tablespoons lemon juice
topping
1/2 cup brown sugar
2/3 cup rolled oats
1/4 cup plain (all-purpose) flour
90g (3 oz) butter, softened
1 teaspoon ground cinnamon

Preheat the oven to 180°C (350°F). Combine the plums, strawberries, sugar, cinnamon and lemon juice. Divide the mixture between 4 ramekins*.
To make the topping, combine the sugar, rolled oats, flour, butter and cinnamon. Pile the oat mixture on top of the fruit. Place the ramekins in the oven and bake for 25 minutes or until the topping is golden and crisp, and the fruit is soft. Serve warm or cold with vanilla bean ice cream. Makes 4.

marsala peaches with mascarpone

1/3 cup (2¾ fl oz) marsala
2 tablespoons brown sugar
2 tablespoons orange juice
4 peaches, halved
150g (5 oz) mascarpone*
1½ tablespoons icing (confectioner's) sugar
3 tablespoons marsala, extra

Combine the marsala, sugar and orange juice, and mix until the sugar is dissolved. Pour over the peaches and allow to macerate for 20 minutes.
Combine the mascarpone and icing sugar, and mix until smooth. Place the peaches and marinade in a preheated hot frying pan and cook for 2–3 minutes each side or until the peaches are golden.
To serve, place the peaches on a plate with a spoonful of mascarpone. Make a small indentation in the mascarpone and fill with the extra marsala. Pour the pan juices over the peaches and serve. Serves 4.

tamarillos soaked in sauternes

marsala peaches with mascarpone

autumn plum and strawberry crumbles

menu ideas

impromptu dinner for 4

spaghetti with lemon, chilli, garlic and rocket
marsala peaches with mascarpone

FOOD PREP
For the main, serve spaghetti with lemon, chilli, garlic and
rocket with bread. Finish with a really simple dessert of grilled
(broiled) fruit such as marsala peaches with mascarpone. You
can swap the peaches for pears or any other fruit good for
grilling (broiling). If you are hard pressed finding mascarpone
at short notice, serve thick cream or good-quality ready-made
ice cream.

LIQUID SUGGESTIONS
Quickly fill glasses with sparkling wine or a lively, refreshing
white wine. If you have a few marinated olives in the fridge,
put them on a platter. The spicy pasta is best served with a
fresh, crisp sauvignon blanc, semillon or blend of these. Top
off the peaches with a good, sweet, chilled dessert wine.

school night dinner for 6

rocket and parmesan flatbread salad
lamb with garlic mash
tamarillos soaked in sauternes

FOOD PREP
Start with something simple and light such as the rocket
(arugula) and parmesan flatbread salad (x 1½). If you have
time, make the flatbreads beforehand and store them in an
airtight container. For mains, try the lamb cutlets with garlic
mash (x 1½) and, if you remember, marinate the cutlets the
morning before the dinner. Place a large bowl of steamed
spinach with lots of cracked black pepper and lemon juice in
the middle of the table. Finish with the tamarillos soaked in
sauternes for dessert. Serve the tamarillos chilled in the hotter
months and warm in the colder.

LIQUID SUGGESTIONS
The peppery rocket (arugula) salad could stand up to a lightly
wooded chardonnay, but I would rather serve it with a
sauvignon blanc. The mustard lamb could be matched with
a cabernet sauvignon or shiraz. Serve dessert with a sweet
dessert wine with strong fruit and honey undertones.

fast dinner for 8

roast fennel and olive salad
jasmine rice pilaf with salt-roasted chicken
tamarillos soaked in sauternes or autumn plum
  and strawberry crumbles

FOOD PREP
The roast fennel and olive salad (double the recipe) is a great
starter that you can prepare ahead of time. You can serve it
cold or warm the vegetables in the oven. The jasmine rice
pilaf with salt-roasted chicken (double the recipe) is easy to
cook in a larger quantity. Serve the rice with steamed green
or snake beans. For dessert, choose between the tamarillos
and the plum and strawberry crumbles, which can both be
made in advance.

LIQUID SUGGESTIONS
A full-bodied wooded chardonnay or a gutsy pinot noir would
be great with the salad. A different combination or the same
wines could be served with the main. With dessert, serve a
late-harvest or a botrytis-affected riesling.

busy person's dinner for 6

mint couscous with fried tomatoes
sesame-crusted ocean trout
autumn plum and strawberry crumbles

FOOD PREP
For the starter, prepare the couscous beforehand without
adding the mint. All you have to do when the guests arrive is
fry the tomatoes and heat the couscous. For the mains, the
sesame-crusted ocean trout with greens not only looks great
but has a wonderful blend of flavours. Finish with cheeses
and fruit, or try the plum and strawberry crumbles if you have
time. Shop the day before and pick up the trout on the way
home on the day of your dinner.

LIQUID SUGGESTIONS
A semillon or sauvignon blanc or blend of these would suit
the lemony zing of the couscous. An aged chardonnay or
semillon or light, peppery pinot noir would complement the
complexity of the salmon. With dessert, try a liqueur muscat
or tokay, or an aged port.

country dinner

basics

Having a small selection of good-quality equipment will make life in the kitchen a whole lot easier. There is no need to have every piece of cooking equipment as well as the kitchen sink or that is exactly where you will spend most of your time—at the kitchen sink. Remember, when purchasing kitchen equipment, the price often reflects the quality and durability of the utensil.

baking dishes and tins

Be wise and buy a quality baking dish first go. A good solid baking dish with ample sides is a must. The same rule goes for cake tins. Cheap cake tins can warp, rust and buckle. Purchase a few cake tins and removable-base tart tins and dry them in a warm oven after cleaning.

knives

A basic set is all you need. Purchase knives with a reputable brand name and solid, riveted handles. One medium- and one large-sized cook's knife for chopping, one small paring knife and one serrated knife make a basic set. You could add to this with a cleaver, and a boning or filleting knife. The only other must-have is a steel to keep your knives sharp.

pots and saucepans

Invest in a set of pots and saucepans that will last you a good 20 years or so. Select a range of saucepans from small through medium to large. You may also wish to have a stockpot large enough to boil up a good quantity of stock or soup. Choose saucepans with heavy bases that contain a layer of copper or aluminium for good conduction of heat.

frying pans

A small, usually non-stick, frying pan for omelettes or pancakes and a large, heavy-based frying pan will cover most tasks. I prefer to have at least one non-stick frying pan so I can cook more delicate things easily.

conical sieves, colanders

A fine conical sieve is great for straining sauces or pasta. Use colanders for draining the contents of a pot or for washing greens.

frying pans

pots and saucepans

knives

baking dish and cake tins

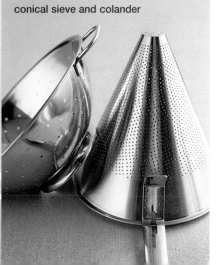

conical sieve and colander

veal cutlets with fried quince

roast herb lamb with apples

veal cutlets with fried quince

2 tablespoons oil
2 tablespoons sage leaves
cracked black pepper
4 thick veal cutlets
2 tablespoons butter
1 quince, peeled, cored and sliced
1/2 cup (4 fl oz) water

Preheat the oven to 180°C (350°F). Heat the oil in a frying pan over high heat. Add the sage and pepper and cook for 1 minute. Add the cutlets and cook for 1 minute each side or until the veal is golden and sealed. Place the cutlets in a baking dish and pour over the pan juices.
Heat the butter in a frying pan over medium heat. Add the quince slices and cook for 2 minutes each side. Add the water to the pan, cover and cook for 5 minutes or until the water has been absorbed. Place the quince slices in the baking dish with the cutlets. Cover the dish and bake for 10–15 minutes or until the veal is cooked to your liking. Serve with the fried quinces, and buttered and peppered broad (fava) beans. Serves 4.

roast herb lamb with apples

1 large leg lamb, tunnel boned with shank bone left in■
8 sprigs thyme
3 red onions, halved
1 tablespoon oil
3 green cooking apples, halved
stuffing
1 tablespoon oil
2 onions, chopped
2 tablespoons oregano leaves
2 tablespoons thyme leaves
3 cups fresh breadcrumbs
3 tablespoons seeded mustard

Preheat the oven to 200°C (400°F). To make the stuffing, place the oil in a frying pan over medium heat. Add the onions and cook for 4 minutes or until golden. Add the oregano and thyme and cook for 1 minute. Combine the onion mixture, breadcrumbs and mustard.
Press the stuffing into the tunnel of the lamb leg. Place the thyme sprigs around the outside of the lamb and tie with string to secure. Place in a baking dish with the red onions. Brush the onions with oil.
Bake the lamb for 25 minutes. Add the apples to the baking dish and cook for 25 minutes or until the lamb is cooked to your liking, and the apples and onions are very soft. Slice the lamb and serve with the baked onions and apples. Serves 4.
■ Ask your butcher to do this for you.

roast garlic chicken with artichoke mash

2 whole heads garlic, unpeeled
1 tablespoon olive oil
4 single chicken breasts on the bone, skin removed
cracked black pepper
Jerusalem artichoke mash
750g (1 1/2 lb) Jerusalem artichokes
3 mashing potatoes, peeled and chopped
1/4 cup (2 fl oz) cream (pouring or single)
2 tablespoons butter
sea salt and cracked black pepper

Preheat the oven to 200°C (400°F). Place the garlic in a baking dish and sprinkle with the oil. Bake for 20 minutes or until golden and soft. Squeeze the soft cloves from their skins and spread the garlic over the flesh of the chicken. Sprinkle over some pepper and place the chicken in a baking dish, cover, reduce the oven temperature to 150°C (300°F) and bake for 30 minutes or until tender.
To make the artichoke mash, place a saucepan of water over high heat and allow to rapidly simmer. Peel the artichokes and immediately drop them into the simmering water, to stop discolouration. Add the potatoes and simmer for 8–12 minutes or until the vegetables are tender. Drain. Place the cream and butter in a saucepan and heat until almost simmering. Pour the hot cream mixture over the vegetables and mash with salt and pepper until smooth. To serve, place the mash on plates and top with the roast chicken. Serve with steamed beans. Serves 4.

simple roast tomato soup

14 ripe tomatoes, halved
1 head garlic
2 brown onions
4 cups (32 fl oz) vegetable stock*
3 tablespoons chopped basil
2 tablespoons chopped mint
cracked black pepper and sea salt

Preheat the oven to 160°C (315°F). Place the tomatoes, garlic and onions on a baking tray. Bake for 45 minutes or until the tomatoes are very soft, and the garlic and onions are golden.
Remove the garlic and onions from their skins, and chop the onion. Place the garlic and onions in a saucepan over medium heat for 3 minutes. Process the onion mixture, tomatoes and half the stock in a food processor or blender until the mixture is roughly chopped.
Return the soup to the saucepan. Add the remaining stock, the basil, mint, salt and pepper. Allow the soup to simmer for 5 minutes. Serves 4 to 6 as a starter.

roast garlic chicken with artichoke mash

simple roast tomato soup

soft polenta with red wine roast beef

braised pickled lamb shanks

soft polenta with red wine roast beef

600g (1¼ lb) piece Scotch or eye fillet

2 cups (16 fl oz) red wine

1 tablespoon cracked black pepper

3 tablespoons chopped rosemary

3 tablespoons chopped lemon thyme

1 tablespoon crushed juniper berries■

soft polenta

1 litre (32 fl oz) hot water

2 cups (16 fl oz) milk

1¼ cups polenta

sea salt and cracked black pepper

85g (3 oz) butter

½ cup grated parmesan cheese

Preheat the oven to 150°C (300°F). Trim the beef of any fat or sinew. Place in a shallow dish with the red wine and allow to marinate for 2 hours, turning once. Drain the marinade and pat the beef dry. Combine the pepper, rosemary, thyme and juniper berries. Roll the beef in the herb mixture to coat. Place the beef in a baking dish and bake for 45 minutes or until cooked to your liking.

To make the polenta, place the water and milk in a heavy-based saucepan over medium heat and bring to a simmer. Slowly pour the polenta into the water while whisking to combine. Reduce the heat to as low as possible. Cover and cook the polenta, stirring occasionally with a wooden spoon so the polenta doesn't stick to the base of the pan, for 20–25 minutes. Stir through the salt, pepper, butter and parmesan.

To serve, place the polenta on plates. Slice the beef and place slices on the polenta. Serves 4.

■Available from speciality food stores and some delicatessens and health food stores.

roast vegetable risotto

750g (1½ lb) orange sweet potato (kumara), peeled and chopped

5 roma tomatoes*

2 leeks, halved

2–3 tablespoons olive or herb oil

2 tablespoons lemon thyme leaves

cracked black pepper

risotto

4–4½ cups (32–36 fl oz) vegetable* or chicken stock*

1 cup (8 fl oz) white wine

1 tablespoon oil

2 cups arborio (risotto)* rice

1 tablespoon rosemary leaves

2 teaspoons grated lemon rind

½ cup grated parmesan cheese

sea salt and cracked black pepper

Preheat the oven to 200°C (400°F). Place the sweet potato, tomatoes and leeks in a baking dish. Drizzle with olive oil and sprinkle with the lemon thyme and pepper. Prick the tomatoes with a fork, place the vegetables in the oven and bake for 35 minutes or until golden and soft.

To make the risotto, place the stock and wine in a saucepan over medium heat and allow to slowly simmer. Heat the oil in a large saucepan over medium heat. Add the rice, rosemary and lemon rind, and cook for 3–4 minutes or until the rice is transparent. Add a cup of the stock mixture to the rice and stir until the liquid has been absorbed. Continue adding the stock, a cup at a time, stirring until the liquid has been absorbed. When all the stock has been used, the rice should be soft and creamy. If the rice is a little hard, add some boiling water. Stir through the parmesan, salt and pepper.

To serve, place the risotto on plates and top with the roast vegetables and extra parmesan and pepper. Serves 4 to 6.

roast vegetable risotto

veal roasted on herbs with sugar-roasted parsnips

wheat and rye bread

veal roasted on herbs with sugar-roasted parsnips

2 heads garlic

olive oil

1 kg (2 lb) standing rib or veal rack

6 bay leaves

8 sprigs rosemary

8 sprigs oregano

2 cups (16 fl oz) white wine

sugar-roasted parsnips

750g (1½ lb) small parsnips, peeled

2 tablespoons oil

3 tablespoons brown sugar

2 tablespoons butter

Preheat the oven to 200°C (400°F). Place the garlic in a baking dish, sprinkle with a little oil and bake for 20 minutes or until golden and soft. Squeeze the garlic cloves from their skins. Spread the garlic flesh over the veal.

Place the bay leaves, rosemary and oregano in a pile in a baking dish and pour the wine over. Place the veal on top of the herbs and bake for 35–45 minutes or until the veal is cooked to your liking.

While the veal is cooking, halve the parsnips and place in a baking dish with the oil. Bake for 20 minutes, then sprinkle over the sugar and dot with butter. Cook for a further 10 minutes, shaking the dish to coat the parsnips with sugar.

To serve, slice the veal and place on plates with the sugar-roasted parsnips. Serves 4.

braised pickled lamb shanks

12 small pearl or small brown onions

3 cloves garlic, peeled

1 tablespoon juniper berries■

2 teaspoons shredded lemon rind

8 pickled lamb shanks■■

4 cups (32 fl oz) beef stock*

1 cup (8 fl oz) red wine

8 very small parsnips, peeled

4 roma tomatoes,* peeled

⅓ cup chopped flat-leaf parsley

Preheat the oven to 180°C (350°F). Place the onions, garlic, juniper berries, lemon rind, lamb shanks, stock, wine, parsnips and tomatoes in a large baking dish. Cover and bake for 45 minutes. Turn the shanks, cover and bake for 30 minutes or until tender. Serve the shanks in deep bowls with some pan broth and lots of flat-leaf parsley. Serves 4.

■ Available from speciality food stores and some delicatessens and health food stores.

■■ Ask your butcher to put some lamb shanks in brine solution, or pickle them, for 1–2 days.

wheat and rye bread

1½ cups (12 fl oz) warm water

2½ teaspoons active dry yeast

1 cup plain (all-purpose) flour

½ cup rye flour

½ cup wholemeal plain (all-purpose) flour

1 teaspoon active dry yeast, extra

1 cup (8 fl oz) warm water, extra

3½–4 cups plain (all-purpose) flour, extra

1 cup wholemeal plain (all-purpose) flour, extra

½ cup coarsely cracked wheat

1 tablespoon sea salt

Place the water and yeast in a bowl and allow to stand until the mixture has a foamy top. Combine the plain, rye and wholemeal flours and mix into the yeast mixture until smooth. Cover the bowl with a damp tea towel and allow to stand for 1 hour or until the mixture has doubled in size. Place the mixture in the bowl of an electric mixer fitted with a dough hook. Combine the extra yeast and water, and allow to stand for 5 minutes.

While the motor is running, add the extra yeast mixture, extra plain and wholemeal flours, the cracked wheat and salt to the bowl. Allow the dough hook to make the mixture into dough and then knead with the dough hook for a further 10 minutes. (The dough may appear to be tacky, but the wheat will absorb the moisture during the proving* process.)

Cover the dough and allow it to prove* and double in size for about 1½–2 hours. Place the dough on a lightly floured surface and knead lightly. Shape the dough into a tight loaf and allow it to prove* for 1 hour.

To bake, preheat a baking stone or a few terracotta tiles in a 220°C (425°F) oven for 20 minutes. Fill a spray bottle with water and spray the oven walls to create steam, then shut the door quickly. Make a few slashes in the top of the bread and slide it onto the preheated stone or tiles. Spray the oven walls with water again and shut the door quickly. Reduce the heat to 200°C (400°F) and bake the bread for 1 hour or until the crust is a deep golden colour and the bread sounds hollow when tapped. Serve the bread warm with the best quality butter you can find. Makes 1 large loaf.

baked quince with quince panna cotta

steamed persimmon pudding

baked quince with quince panna cotta

4 quinces, peeled and halved
3 cups sugar
6 cups (48 fl oz) boiling water
1 vanilla bean
quince panna cotta
2 cups (16 fl oz) cream (single or pouring)
½ cup (4 fl oz) milk
3 teaspoons gelatine
¼ cup (2 fl oz) boiling water

Preheat the oven to 150°C (300°F). Place the quinces in a large baking dish. Combine the sugar and water, and mix to dissolve the sugar. Add the sugar and water mixture and the vanilla bean to the baking dish. Cover and bake, turning the quinces twice, for 4–5 hours or until a blushing pink colour and soft.
To make the panna cotta, remove 1 cup (8 fl oz) of simmering liquid from the quinces in the baking dish and place in a saucepan. Bring to the boil and simmer until ½ cup (4 fl oz) remains. Add the cream and milk and allow to heat. Sprinkle the gelatine over the boiling water and stir to dissolve. Add the gelatine mixture to the cream mixture. Pour into 8 small, greased ramekins* and refrigerate for 4 hours or until set.
Before serving, heat the quinces gently in the remaining syrup in the oven. Place the quinces on plates and unmould the panna cotta next to them. Serves 8.

steamed persimmon pudding

1½ cups plain (all-purpose) flour
2 teaspoons baking powder
60g (2 oz) butter, softened
2 eggs
⅔ cup sugar
3 tablespoons golden syrup
1½ cups persimmon puree

Place the flour, baking powder, butter, eggs, sugar, golden syrup and persimmon puree in the bowl of an electric mixer and beat for 2–3 minutes or until well combined. Pour into a greased pudding mould, cover with paper and aluminium foil and tie tightly with string, or cover with a tight-fitting lid. Place the pudding mould in a large saucepan of boiling water and allow the water to come three-quarters of the way up the sides of the pudding mould. Boil the pudding for 2 hours or until cooked when tested with a skewer. Allow the pudding to stand for 5 minutes before inverting onto a serving plate and serving with persimmon slices and thick, honey-flavoured cream. Serves 8.

fig and brioche pudding

12 large slices brioche
5 figs, thickly sliced
2 cups (16 fl oz) cream (single or pouring)
2 cups (16 fl oz) milk
3 eggs
⅓ cup sugar
1 teaspoon vanilla extract
demerara sugar*

Preheat the oven to 180°C (350°F). Alternately layer the brioche and figs in a greased 5-cup capacity ovenproof dish. Place the cream, milk, eggs, sugar and vanilla extract in a bowl and whisk to combine. Pour over the brioche and figs and allow to stand for 5 minutes. Sprinkle over some demerara sugar and place the dish in a baking dish. Fill the baking dish with enough hot water to come halfway up the sides of the inner dish.
Bake for 25 minutes or until the pudding is set. Serve hot with scoops of vanilla bean ice cream. Serves 4 to 6.

lime curd tarts with pomegranate

1 quantity (350g or 12 oz) sweet shortcrust pastry*
1 pomegranate
lime curd
90g (3 oz) butter
¾ cup caster (superfine) sugar
½ cup (4 fl oz) lime juice
2 eggs, lightly beaten

Preheat the oven to 200°C (400°F). Roll out the pastry on a lightly floured surface until 2mm (⅛ in) thick. Cut into circles to fit 12 x 6cm (2½ in) tart tins. Prick the pastry bases, line with non-stick baking paper and fill with pastry weights or rice. Bake the shells for 4 minutes. Remove the paper and weights, and cook the shells for a further 4 minutes or until golden.
To make the lime curd, place the butter, sugar, lime juice and eggs in a heatproof bowl over rapidly simmering water. Stir the mixture until it thickens, then cover and refrigerate until cold.
To serve, remove the pomegranate seeds from the shell. Spoon the lime curd into the tart shells and top with the pomegranate seeds. Makes 12.

fig and brioche pudding

lime curd tarts with pomegranate

menu ideas

big family dinner for 8

simple roast tomato soup
wheat and rye bread
roast herb lamb with apples
steamed persimmon pudding

FOOD PREP
Make the simple roast tomato soup (double the recipe) up to
1 day beforehand. Heat and serve it with the wheat and rye
bread or buy some good-quality bread to accompany the
soup. For mains, 1 large or 2 small quantities of the roast herb
lamb with apples, with a few extra onions and apples in the
pan, will be enough to go around. Place the roast in the oven
before serving the soup. Serve the lamb with some roasted
root vegetables or steamed beans and broccoli. Steamed
persimmon pudding is a warming and comforting dessert.

LIQUID SUGGESTIONS
Choose a well-flavoured pinot noir or a cabernet sauvignon for
the soup. Continue with a cabernet sauvignon with the lamb or
move on to a shiraz. Serve dessert with a sweet sticky dessert
wine served at room temperature or just quickly chilled. Or you
could skip the sticky and have a coffee and a port.

winter dinner for 6

roast vegetable risotto
braised pickled lamb shanks
fig and brioche pudding

FOOD PREP
The risotto makes a good, hearty starter with the braised
pickled lamb shanks (x 1½) and a large bowl of steamed
greens to follow. The shanks can be made a day ahead and
reheated. To finish, offer small portions of fig and brioche
pudding. Arrange the brioche and figs in the baking dish
ahead of time and pour over the custard, which can also be
prepared ahead of time, just before baking.

LIQUID SUGGESTIONS
To start, a well-rounded cabernet sauvignon or merlot blend
makes a good accompaniment for the risotto. Move on to
a spicy shiraz with the shanks and a liqueur muscat with
the pudding.

cosy dinner for 2

simple roast tomato soup
veal roasted on herbs with sugar-roasted parsnips
baked quince with quince panna cotta

FOOD PREP
Serve the simple roast tomato soup with some warm bread
for starters. Freeze the leftover soup for a Sunday afternoon.
Follow the soup with the veal roasted on herbs with sugar-
roasted parsnips. The baked quince with quince panna cotta
will top off the evening well and can be made a day ahead.

LIQUID SUGGESTIONS
The robust and well-flavoured soup would be good with a
rich pinot noir or with a cabernet sauvignon. Serve the same
wine with the main or change to a merlot blend with lots of
flavour. The dessert would suit a chilled late-harvest riesling.

sunday lunch for 4

soft polenta with red wine roast beef or roast garlic chicken
  with artichoke mash
baked quince with quince panna cotta

FOOD PREP
Skip the starters or serve warm bread with a few pastes or
spreads. You could serve the soft polenta with red wine roast
beef or the roast garlic chicken with artichoke mash for mains
and then the baked quince with quince panna cotta, which
can be made well in advance, for dessert.

LIQUID SUGGESTIONS
Serve a light pinot when your guests arrive to get those
tastebuds ready for a well-flavoured, hearty lunch. Serve a
big-flavoured cabernet sauvignon or shiraz with the beef or, if
you choose the chicken, a grenache blend or a well-flavoured
pinot noir. Serve the quinces with a liqueur tokay or a smooth
and sticky dessert wine.

red carpet dining

basics

It's special-occasion time, so polish up your best glasses and clean the silver. Don't be afraid to pull out the family heirlooms. Formal dining occasions are becoming increasingly rare so, when you do roll out the red carpet, do it with simple style and as much finesse as possible. For a smooth performance, prepare as much of the food as you can ahead of time, set and dress the table in advance, and have the drinks and pre-dinner morsels ready to serve when your guests arrive.

napkins and napery

Use large thick white napkins and napery, or go for rich colours to accessorise and add variety, colour and warmth to your table.

glasses

I think it is more important to have good-quality glasses than different glasses for every occasion. Red and white wine can be served from the same generous wine glass. It makes more sense to buy a larger set of one type of glass. Clear glasses from the table and rinse them before serving different wine in the same glass. Dessert wine, port, liqueur or shot glasses are also handy to have.

cutlery

Just like fashion, plain, classic, good-quality cutlery will serve you well. Cutlery should balance easily in the hand and be effortless to use.

crockery

White crockery is always a safe option and makes food look appetising and fresh. Co-ordinate large serving ware in white or with colours to match.

table centre

A table centre can not only be beautiful but is also a great way to scent a room—whether it is a bowl of quinces or ruby grapefruit, which give off their natural fragrance, or flowers.

cutlery

napkins

table centre

Please sit here

your place

crockery

glasses

157

potato galettes with soft quail eggs

oysters with cucumber salad

potato galettes with soft quail eggs

6 quail eggs
60g (2 oz) salmon roe
potato galettes
8 kipfler (finger) potatoes, peeled and thinly sliced
olive oil
1 cup grated parmesan cheese
cracked black pepper
1 leek, shredded

Preheat the oven to 200°C (400°F). To make the potato galettes, brush the slices of potato with a little oil, and sprinkle with parmesan and pepper. Form 6 piles of potato slices and top with the leek. Place the piles on a baking tray lined with non-stick baking paper and bake for 20–25 minutes or until the potatoes are golden and crisp. To serve, place the quail eggs in simmering water for 45 seconds to 1 minute, then peel. Place the galettes on warm plates and top with a halved quail egg and some salmon roe. Serves 6 as a starter.

oysters with cucumber salad

36 freshly shucked oysters
cucumber salad
1 Lebanese cucumber, shredded
1/4 cup chervil* leaves
2 tablespoons lime juice
cracked black pepper

To make the cucumber salad, combine the cucumber, chervil, lime juice and pepper.
To serve, lift each oyster from its shell and place a spoonful of cucumber salad under it. Serves 4 to 6 as a starter.

chicken roasted on tomatoes and eggplant

6 roma tomatoes,* halved
2 small eggplants (aubergines), halved and scored
olive oil
pepper
2 tablespoons oregano leaves
2 tablespoons butter
1 tablespoon lemon juice
4 chicken breast fillets, skin on

Preheat the oven to 180°C (350°F). Place the tomatoes and eggplants in a baking dish, drizzle with oil, and sprinkle with pepper and oregano leaves. Bake for 35 minutes or until the vegetables are soft.
Heat the butter and lemon juice in a frying pan over high heat. Add the chicken and cook, skin-side down, for 3–4 minutes or until well browned. Place the chicken on the tomatoes and eggplants and spoon over the lemon butter. Reduce the heat to 150°C (300°F) and bake for 15 minutes or until the chicken is cooked through. Serve with pan juices. Serves 4.

crispy duck lasagne

8 small wonton wrappers*
oil for deep-frying
spiced duck
1 Chinese barbecue duck*
1 tablespoon oil
1 leek, shredded
120g (4 oz) fresh shiitake mushrooms*
2 teaspoons shredded orange rind
1/4 cup (2 fl oz) Chinese cooking (shao hsing) wine
   (see page 32)

To prepare the spiced duck, remove all the meat from the duck and slice. Set aside.
Heat the oil in a frying pan or wok over high heat. Add the leek and cook for 6 minutes or until golden. Add the mushrooms, orange rind and wine and cook for 2 minutes. Add the duck and cook for 2 minutes or until heated through.
Cook the wontons, a few at a time, in the hot oil until golden and crisp. Drain on paper towel. Place a wonton wrapper on 4 individual serving plates. Top each wonton with a spoonful of duck mixture. Top this with another wonton wrapper. Serve immediately. Serves 4 as a starter, or with steamed greens as a main meal.

chicken roasted on tomatoes and eggplant

olive-crusted lamb with couscous salad

crispy duck lasagne

spiced tuna with udon and dashi

olive-crusted lamb with couscous salad

750g (1½ lb) lamb backstrap or eye of loin
½ cup green olives
2 teaspoons grated lemon rind
2 tablespoons chopped flat-leaf parsley
2 tablespoons chopped mint
couscous salad
1½ cups couscous
1½ cups (12 fl oz) boiling vegetable stock*
2 tablespoons olive oil
2 onions, sliced
200g (6½ oz) green beans, trimmed
2 tablespoons chopped flat-leaf parsley
⅓ cup caper berries*
2 tablespoons lemon juice

Preheat the oven to 160°C (315°F). Trim the lamb of any fat or sinew. Finely chop the olives and combine with the lemon rind, parsley and mint. Spread over the lamb and place in an oiled baking dish. Bake for 30 minutes or until the lamb is cooked to your liking.

To make the couscous salad, place the couscous and stock in a bowl, cover and set aside until the stock is absorbed. Heat the oil in a frying pan over high heat. Add the onions and cook for 5 minutes or until golden. Add the beans, parsley, caper berries and lemon juice and cook for 4 minutes. Add the couscous and heat through.

To serve, place the couscous on plates. Slice the lamb thickly, place slices on top of the couscous and serve with lemon wedges. Serves 4.

rosemary lamb cutlets with truffle oil mash

12 lamb cutlets
12 sprigs rosemary
1 tablespoon oil
1 tablespoon seeded mustard
truffle oil mash
8 mashing potatoes
50g (1¾ oz) butter
3 tablespoons cream (single or pouring)
sea salt
truffle-infused oil■

Trim the cutlets and tie a sprig of rosemary around each one. Combine the oil and mustard, and brush over the lamb.

To make the truffle oil mash, peel and chop the potatoes. Place in a saucepan of boiling water and cook until soft. Drain. Place the butter and cream in the pan and cook until the butter is melted and the cream is hot. Add the potatoes and mash until smooth. Season with salt.

To cook the lamb, preheat a frying pan or grill (broiler) over high heat. Add the cutlets and cook for 1–2 minutes each side or until cooked to your liking.

To serve, place the mash on plates and drizzle with truffle oil. Place the cutlets on the plates with the mash. Serve with steamed asparagus. Serves 4.

■ Available from speciality food stores and some delicatessens. Truffle oil has an intense flavour, so use sparingly.

rosemary lamb cutlets with truffle oil mash

slow-roasted spice crust salmon

squid ink pasta with salmon and roe

spiced tuna with udon and dashi

3 tablespoons mild chilli oil
2 tablespoons lime juice
2 tablespoons balsamic vinegar
1 tablespoon shredded ginger
1 tablespoon chopped coriander (cilantro)
4 tuna steaks
200g (6½ oz) udon noodles*
3 cups (24 fl oz) dashi broth*
2 green onions (scallions), sliced

Combine the chilli oil, lime juice, balsamic vinegar, ginger and coriander. Place the tuna in the marinade and refrigerate for 2 hours, turning once.
To serve, heat the udon noodles in boiling water. Drain and place in bowls. Top with the hot dashi broth and onions. Preheat a frying pan or grill (broiler) over high heat. Cook the tuna for 30 seconds to 1 minute each side or until well seared. Place the tuna on top of the noodles and broth. Serves 4.

slow-roasted spice crust salmon

650g (1 lb 5 oz) salmon fillet, skin removed
2 tablespoons coriander seeds
cracked black pepper
3 tablespoons olive oil
1½ cups (12 fl oz) cream (single or pouring)
1 kaffir lime* leaf
1 tablespoon coriander (cilantro) leaves
1 toasted nori* sheet, finely sliced
caviar for serving (optional)

Preheat the oven to 120°C (230°F). Remove any visible bones from the salmon. Wash and pat dry. Toast the coriander seeds in a frying pan over medium heat for 3–5 minutes or until aromatic. Crush the coriander seeds with a mortar and pestle, and spread over the salmon. Cut the salmon into 4 pieces and sprinkle lightly with pepper. Place the oil and salmon in a baking dish. Bake for 20 minutes or until the salmon has changed colour and is cooked medium.
While the salmon is cooking, place the cream, kaffir lime leaf and coriander leaves in a saucepan and allow to simmer until reduced by at least half.
To serve, spoon a little of the sauce onto serving plates, top with a piece of salmon, sprinkle with the nori slices and place a spoonful of caviar on the side. Serve with steamed greens. Serves 4 as a starter.

squid ink pasta with salmon and roe

400g (13 oz) fresh squid ink pasta
90g (3 oz) butter
3 tablespoons lime juice
2 tablespoons chervil* sprigs
400g (13 oz) salmon fillet, thickly sliced
cracked black pepper
100g (3½ oz) salmon roe

Place the pasta in a saucepan of boiling water and cook for 5–6 minutes or until al dente. Drain. While the pasta is cooking, place the butter and lime juice in a frying pan over high heat and cook until the mixture is bubbling. Add the chervil and salmon and cook the salmon for 30 seconds each side or until well sealed.
Place the pasta on warm plates and top with the salmon, pan juices, pepper and salmon roe. Serve immediately. Serves 6 as a starter or 4 as a main meal.

grilled scampi tails on lemon and chive risotto

8 green (raw) scampi (langoustine) or fresh-water yabbies
60g (2 oz) butter, melted
1 tablespoon small sage leaves
cracked black pepper
lemon and chive risotto
4½ cups (36 fl oz) vegetable* or chicken stock*
1 cup (8 fl oz) dry white wine
2 tablespoons oil
2 teaspoons grated lemon rind
2 cups arborio (risotto) rice*
3 tablespoons lemon juice
¼ cup snipped chives
½ cup grated parmesan cheese

To make the lemon and chive risotto, place the stock and wine in a saucepan over medium heat, and allow to slowly simmer. Place the oil in a large saucepan over medium heat. Add the lemon rind and rice and cook for 1 minute. Add the hot stock mixture to the rice, a few cups at a time, stirring frequently so the rice doesn't stick, and the risotto develops a creamy texture. Continue adding the stock until all the liquid has been absorbed and the rice is tender. If the rice is not tender, add a little boiling water. Stir the lemon juice, chives and parmesan through the rice.
While the risotto is cooking, prepare the scampi. Cut the scampi tails in half and remove the claws. Place the tails and claws on a baking tray and sprinkle with the butter, sage and pepper. Place the tray under a preheated hot grill (broiler) and cook for 2–3 minutes or until cooked.
To serve, place the risotto on plates and top with the grilled scampi. Serves 4.

grilled scampi tails on lemon and chive risotto

caramelised vanilla risotto pudding

2 cups (16 fl oz) water
2 cups (16 fl oz) milk
2 tablespoons butter
1 cup arborio (risotto) rice*
1 vanilla bean*, split
3 tablespoons sugar
1 teaspoon vanilla extract
1 cup (8 fl oz) cream (single or pouring)
2 egg yolks
extra sugar
warm poached blood plums to serve

Place the water and milk in a saucepan over moderate heat and allow to simmer.
Heat the butter in a saucepan over moderate heat. Add the rice and cook for 3 minutes. Add the vanilla bean. Add the milk mixture to the rice 1 cup (8 fl oz) at a time, stirring occasionally, until the liquid has been absorbed. Remove the vanilla bean and stir the sugar and vanilla extract through the rice. Whisk together the cream and egg yolks. Stir into the risotto and cook until the cream has been absorbed.
To serve, place the risotto on plates and sprinkle with the extra sugar. Heat a large metal cook's spoon or brûlée iron* over high heat. Run the spoon or iron over the sugar until it melts and is golden. Serve the caramelised risotto with poached plums. Serves 4 to 6.

chocolate and raspberry fudgy cake

185g (6 oz) butter
185g (6 oz) dark chocolate, chopped
3 eggs
1/2 teaspoon vanilla extract
1 1/2 cups caster (superfine) sugar
1 2/3 cups plain (all-purpose) flour
3/4 teaspoon baking powder
1/2 cup almond meal
1 cup raspberries

Preheat the oven to 160°C (315°F). Place the butter and chocolate in a saucepan over low heat and stir until melted. Allow to cool slightly.
Place the eggs, vanilla extract and sugar in a bowl and beat until light and thick. Fold through the flour, baking powder, almond meal, chocolate mixture and half the raspberries. Pour the mixture into a 20cm (8 in) round cake tin lined with non-stick baking paper. Sprinkle over the remaining raspberries and bake for 1 hour 40 minutes or until the top of the cake is firm to touch. Allow the cake to cool before cutting, and serve with strong espresso, extra raspberries and thick cream. Serves 8 to 10.

caramelised vanilla risotto pudding

chocolate and raspberry fudgy cake

little lemon curd tarts

1 quantity (350g or 12 oz) sweet shortcrust pastry*
filling
3/4 cup caster (superfine) sugar
3 eggs
3/4 cup (6 fl oz) cream (single or pouring)
1/2 cup (4 fl oz) lemon juice
1 teaspoon grated lemon rind

Preheat the oven to 200°C (400°F). Roll out the pastry
on a lightly floured surface until 2mm (1/8 in) thick. Cut into
6 circles to fit six 1-cup (8 fl oz) capacity muffin tins. Prick
the pastry, line with non-stick baking paper and fill with rice
or baking weights. Bake for 5 minutes. Remove the rice
or weights and paper, and bake the pastry for a further
4 minutes or until light golden.
To make the filling, place the sugar, eggs, cream, lemon
juice and rind in a bowl and mix to combine. Pour the filling
into the tart shells. Reduce the oven heat to 160°C (315°F)
and bake for 20 minutes or until the filling is just set. Allow
the tarts to cool and serve with thick cream and berries.
Serves 6.

ice-cream cones

vanilla bean ice cream
cones
3/4 cup icing (confectioner's) sugar
1 cup plain (all-purpose) flour
3 egg whites
90g (3 oz) butter, melted

Preheat the oven to 180°C (350°F). To make the cones,
combine the icing sugar, flour, egg whites and butter. Allow
to stand for 10 minutes. Take 2 tablespoons of the mixture
and spread into a thin circle on a baking tray lined with
non-stick baking paper. Bake the wafers for 8–10 minutes
or until just beginning to brown on the edges.
Remove the wafers from the tray with a spatula and fold
each one around the handle of a rolling pin to form a cone.
Allow to stand for 1 minute before removing the cone from
the rolling pin.
To serve, fill the cones with vanilla bean ice cream and store
in the freezer or serve immediately. Serves 6 to 8.

little lemon curd tart

ice cream cone

menu ideas

'the in-laws are coming' dinner for 4

oysters with cucumber salad
slow-roasted spice crust salmon
olive-crusted lamb with couscous salad
chocolate and raspberry fudgy cake

FOOD PREP

It's make or break time so be sure to find out what they don't eat. A few oysters with cucumber salad, prepared ahead of time and refrigerated until they arrive, accompanied with a drink should settle everyone comfortably. Follow the oysters with the spice crust salmon and the lamb with couscous salad. For dessert, the chocolate and raspberry fudgy cake is fantastic and can be made a day in advance.

LIQUID SUGGESTIONS

Celebrate your guests' arrival with a dry sparkling white wine, which also goes well with the oysters. The salmon is best served with a lightly wooded chardonnay or semillon, then move on to a spicy pinot noir or a full-bodied cabernet sauvignon. The dessert cake is perfect with a glass of sweet botrytis-affected riesling and a coffee. Don't forget to wrap extra cake for them to take home.

the boss's dinner for 6

oysters with cucumber salad
crispy duck lasagne
rosemary lamb cutlets with truffle oil mash
little lemon curd tarts

FOOD PREP

Serious red carpet time: but don't be too showy or you may find yourself with a salary decrease. Simple and stylish is the way to go. Start with a few oysters with cucumber, prepared the day before and refrigerated until required, and then move on to the duck lasagne (x 1½). Serve mains of rosemary lamb cutlets with mash (x 1½) with a bowl of steamed baby spinach dressed with a squeeze of lemon and a sprinkling of black pepper and parmesan in the middle of the table. Prepare the cutlets and potatoes beforehand and cook when required. Finish with the lemon tarts, which can be made the morning before, and coffee and chocolate truffles. Perfect.

LIQUID SUGGESTIONS

Serve a dry sparkling white to toast your guests' arrival and to accompany the oysters. The duck lasagne is great with a sparkling red (that will surprise them) or a good pinot noir. The rosemary lamb is very full flavoured, so an aged cabernet sauvignon or shiraz is best. The lemon tarts have a zesty tang and are best served with a not-so-sweet dessert wine such as a late-harvest semillon. Finish in the lounge room with coffee, truffles and port.

formal dinner for 8

potato galettes with soft quail eggs
grilled scampi tails on lemon and chive risotto
chicken roasted on tomatoes and eggplant
ice-cream cones

FOOD PREP

Seriously consider whether you really want to have more than 8 people for a formal dinner as glasses, crockery, cutlery and oven space often run short. As an appetiser, the potato galettes with soft quail eggs (double the recipe) are very impressive. Follow this with small serves of the grilled scampi on lemon and chive risotto and, for mains, the chicken roasted on tomatoes and eggplant (double the recipe) is quite easy to cook for 8 people. A dessert of ice-cream cones filled with vanilla bean ice cream, which can be made ahead of time and stored in the freezer, is not only cute but simple.

LIQUID SUGGESTIONS

Serve sparkling dry white wine when your guests arrive, followed by an aged semillon with the potato galettes. Move on to a sauvignon blanc with the risotto and an aged, lightly wooded chardonnay or a pinot noir with the chicken. Serve the ice-cream cones with a liqueur tokay and then coffee with cognac or port.

10

tea party

basics

Tea is an evergreen shrub that grows in mountainous, subtropical to tropical areas. There are thousands of types of tea and the differences are based on where the tea is grown, how it is plucked and how it is processed.

black tea

These teas are fully fermented and black in appearance. Varieties of black tea include darjeeling, assam, ceylon and keemun. When black teas are brewed they have a rich amber colour. During processing, some black teas are smoked for extra flavour.

oolong

Oolong tea is partially fermented—a cross between green tea and black tea. It should have large, rusty brown leaves with silver tips. The tea is fragrant with a distinctive sweet aftertaste.

white tea

White tea is a rare tea found in China. The leaves are not fermented. It is used for special occasions, such as weddings, and is rather expensive. The silver tips stand on end when they are served. Only a few leaves are needed to make a cup of tea.

green tea

Green tea has been made by the Chinese and Japanese for centuries. Green tea is not fermented; it is made by sun-drying the tender tea leaves and then either pan firing them in a special wok or lightly steaming them. Steaming the tea leaves takes away the bitter flavour. The tea leaves should be light green and have a delicate, subtle taste. Some varieties of green tea include gunpowder, lung ching, sencha and gen mai cha.

herbal teas

Although not 'teas' in the true sense of the word, herbal teas (or tissanes) are drunk in the same way. They may be fermented teas combined with the dried fruits, flowers, leaves, roots or stems of plants, or they may be dried herbal combinations. These teas are brewed in the same way as regular tea and are sometimes used as naturopathic remedies. Popular herbal teas include lemongrass, chamomile, peppermint and raspberry.

oolong tea

green tea

white tea or buddha's tears

herbal tea

black tea

little chocolate mud cakes

baby raspberry and coconut cake

mint, lemon and ginger iced tea + banana and palm sugar wontons

candied lemon and lime tart

little chocolate mud cakes

300g (10 oz) dark chocolate, chopped
300g (10 oz) butter
5 eggs
½ cup sugar
¾ cup plain (all-purpose) flour, sifted
¾ teaspoon baking powder

Preheat the oven to 160°C (315°F). Place the chocolate and butter in a saucepan over low heat and stir until smooth. Set aside.
Place the eggs and sugar in a bowl and beat until light and fluffy (about 6 minutes). Fold the egg mixture through the flour, baking powder and chocolate mixture. Pour into 12 paper-lined or well-greased patty tins■ and bake for 25 minutes or until the cakes feel firm to touch. Serve warm with a sprinkling of good-quality cocoa powder. Makes 12.
■ You can also use a greased 23cm (9 in) round cake tin with the base lined with non-stick baking paper. Bake for 45 minutes or until the cake feels firm to touch.

baby raspberry and coconut cakes

125g (4 oz) unsalted butter
¼ cup almond meal
¾ cup desiccated coconut
1⅔ cups icing (confectioner's) sugar, sifted
½ cup plain (all-purpose) flour, sifted
½ teaspoon baking powder
5 egg whites
⅔ cup raspberries, fresh or frozen

Preheat the oven to 180°C (350°F). Place the butter in a saucepan over low heat and cook until a very light golden colour. Place the almond meal, coconut, icing sugar, flour and baking powder in a bowl and mix to combine. Add the egg whites and mix. Add the melted butter and continue to mix until combined.
Pour the mixture into greased small brioche or patty tins. Sprinkle the raspberries over the tops of the cakes. Bake for 12–15 minutes or until golden, springy to touch and moist in the centre. Serve with clotted cream and fruit tea. Makes 10.

mint, lemon and ginger iced tea

4 tablespoons peppermint tea leaves
8–10 slices ginger
½ cup mint leaves
⅔ cup sugar
6 cups (48 fl oz) water
1 cup (8 fl oz) lemon juice
extra ginger slices and mint leaves

Place the tea leaves, ginger, mint and sugar in a bowl. Place the water in a saucepan and bring to the boil. Pour the boiling water over the mixture in the bowl and allow to steep for 8 minutes. Strain.
Stir the lemon juice through the tea and refrigerate for 2 hours or until well chilled. Pour the tea into a chilled jug and add the extra ginger slices and mint leaves. Serve over ice. Makes 6 cups.
Note: this tea is a great body cleanser and pick-me-up.

banana and palm sugar wontons

2 bananas, thickly sliced
2 tablespoons lime juice
½ cup crumbled palm sugar (see page 32)
20 wonton wrappers*
1 tablespoon cornflour (cornstarch)
2 tablespoons water
oil for shallow-frying
icing (confectioner's) sugar
cinnamon

Brush the bananas lightly with the lime juice and toss in the palm sugar. Place a piece of banana on one half of the wonton wrappers. Brush the wonton wrapper edges with the combined cornflour and water. Fold the wonton wrappers to enclose the banana and squeeze the edges to seal.
Heat the oil in a frying pan until hot. Fry the wontons for 1–2 minutes each side or until golden. Drain on paper towel. When the wontons are cool enough to touch, toss them in the combined icing sugar and cinnamon to coat. Serve warm with tea. Makes 20.

wild raspberry and lime tea + nectarine and basil iced tea

candied lemon and lime tarts

1 quantity (350g or 12 oz) sweet shortcrust pastry*
filling
2 eggs, lightly beaten
$2/3$ cup ($5^{1}/2$ fl oz) lemon juice
$1/3$ cup ($2^{3}/4$ fl oz) lime juice
1 cup caster (superfine) sugar
2 cups (16 fl oz) cream (single or pouring)
topping
2 cups sugar
1 cup (8 fl oz) water
2 lemons, sliced
3 limes, sliced

Preheat the oven to 200°C (400°F). Roll out the pastry on a lightly floured surface until 3mm ($1/8$ in) thick. Cut to fit eight 10cm (4 in) deep tart tins. Prick the pastry shells with a fork and line with non-stick baking paper. Fill the shells with rice or baking weights and bake for 5 minutes. Remove the weights or rice and baking paper, and return the shells to the oven for 5 minutes or until the pastry is light golden. To make the topping, place the sugar and water in a large saucepan over low heat and stir gently until the sugar is dissolved. Simmer the sugar syrup for 1 minute. Add the lemon and lime slices to the pan in one layer. Cook over a very low heat for 20 minutes or until the rinds are soft. Do not boil. Place the slices on non-stick baking paper and allow to cool and set.
To make the filling, combine the eggs, lemon and lime juice, sugar and cream. Pour the mixture into the pastry shells and bake at 160°C (315°F) for 10 minutes or until the filling is beginning to set. Top the tarts with the slices of candied lemon and lime, and return to the oven. Bake for a further 10 minutes or until the filling is just set. Makes 8.

wild raspberry and lime iced tea

5 tablespoons wild raspberry tea leaves■
$4^{1}/2$ cups (36 fl oz) boiling water
$1/2$ cup sugar
$1/3$ cup ($2^{3}/4$ fl oz) lime juice
1 tablespoon shredded lime rind
$1/2$ cup raspberries

Place the tea leaves in the water and allow to steep for 5 minutes. Strain and mix the tea with the sugar, lime juice and lime rind. Before serving, add the raspberries and serve over crushed ice. Makes 4 cups.
■ Available from speciality tea stores.

nectarine and basil iced tea

2 tablespoons darjeeling tea leaves
1 cup basil leaves
2 tablespoons mint leaves
$1/2$ cup sugar
5 cups (40 fl oz) water
4 large nectarines, pureed and sieved
extra nectarines and basil to serve

Place the tea leaves, basil, mint and sugar in a bowl. Place the water in a saucepan and bring to the boil. Pour the boiling water over the mixture in the bowl and allow to steep for 6–7 minutes. Strain. Stir through the pureed nectarine and refrigerate for 2 hours or until well chilled. Pour the tea into a jug with extra nectarine slices and basil leaves, and serve in tall glasses over ice. Serves 6.

ricotta, spinach and parmesan tarts

500g (1 lb) fresh ricotta
$1/3$ cup sour cream
1 egg, lightly beaten
cracked black pepper
pinch freshly grated nutmeg
500g (1 lb) baby English spinach leaves
$1/2$ cup finely grated parmesan cheese
$1/4$ cup chopped toasted pine nuts
1 tablespoon chopped dill

Preheat the oven to 160°C (315°F). Process the ricotta in a food processor until smooth. Place the ricotta, sour cream, egg, pepper and nutmeg in a bowl and mix to combine. Place the spinach in a saucepan of boiling water for 5 seconds, then drain and chop. Squeeze any excess liquid from the spinach.
Stir the spinach, parmesan, pine nuts and dill into the ricotta mixture. Spoon the mixture into greased deep patty tins and bake for 25–30 minutes or until the tarts are firm and golden. Makes 12.

ricotta, spinach and parmesan tarts

winter liquorice tea

green apple and vanilla tea sorbet

winter liquorice tea

5½ cups (44 fl oz) water
3 tablespoons liquorice root tea leaves■
1 tablespoon orange rind strips with white pith
3 tablespoons mint leaves
½ cup (4 fl oz) orange juice
1–2 tablespoons honey

Place the water in a saucepan and bring to the boil.
Remove from the heat and add the tea leaves, orange rind
and mint leaves. Allow to steep for 5 minutes. Strain and
return to the pan. Bring the tea to the boil and add the
orange juice and honey to taste. Serve in warmed glasses.
Serves 4.
■ Available from speciality tea stores and health food stores.

green apple and vanilla tea sorbet

1 cup (8 fl oz) boiling water
3 tablespoons vanilla tea leaves■
4 cups (32 fl oz) fresh green apple juice
2 teaspoons finely grated lemon rind
1 cup sugar

Place the boiling water and tea leaves in a bowl and allow
to steep for 5 minutes. Strain through a fine sieve and place
the tea in a saucepan with 1 cup (8 fl oz) of the apple juice.
Add the lemon rind and sugar to the pan and stir over low
heat until the sugar is dissolved. Add the remaining apple
juice and refrigerate until cold.
Place the mixture in an ice-cream maker and follow the
manufacturer's instructions until the sorbet is frozen and
scoopable. Alternatively, place the mixture in a metal
container and freeze for 1 hour, then whisk and freeze for
another hour. Whisk and repeat. Serves 4 to 6.
■ Available from speciality tea stores.

apple and honey tea cakes

1 tablespoon lemon juice
4 tablespoons demerara sugar*
2 tablespoons butter
3 green apples, peeled and sliced
cake
185g (6 oz) butter
⅔ cup sugar
2 tablespoons honey
1 teaspoon vanilla extract
3 eggs
1½ cups plain (all-purpose) flour, sifted
1 teaspoon baking powder

Preheat the oven to 160°C (315°F). Place the lemon juice,
sugar and butter in a frying pan over high heat. Stir until
the mixture forms a syrup. Add the apples, a few at a time,
and cook for 1 minute each side or until lightly browned.
Set aside.
To make the cake, place the butter, sugar and honey in a
bowl and beat until light and creamy. Add the vanilla and
eggs, one at a time, and beat well. Sift together the flour
and baking powder, and fold into the butter mixture.
Layer the apple slices on the bases of 8 well-greased or
based-lined (with non-stick baking paper) small rectangular
10cm x 5½cm (4 in x 2¼ in) cake tins. Top the apple with
the cake mixture until the tins are three-quarters full. Bake
for 25 minutes or until the cakes are cooked when tested
with a skewer. Invert the cakes onto plates and serve warm
with cream and a pot of hot tea. Makes 8.

tea-soaked little pears

12 small corella* or cocktail pears
1 tablespoon lemongrass* tea leaves
3 tablespoons sugar
1 tablespoon mint leaves
2 cups (16 fl oz) boiling water
2 teaspoons lemon juice

Peel the pears and set aside. Place the lemongrass tea
leaves, sugar, mint and water in a jug and allow to infuse
for 4 minutes. Strain. Place the tea in a saucepan and
heat until boiling. Add the pears and allow to simmer for
8–10 minutes or until soft. Serve the pears warm or chilled
in bowls with the tea. Serves 4 to 6.

tea-soaked little pears

apple and honey tea cakes

menu ideas

summer garden tea party for 10

baby raspberry and coconut cakes
little chocolate mud cakes
apple and honey tea cakes
ricotta, spinach and parmesan tarts
nectarine and basil iced tea

FOOD PREP

A selection of small cakes and morsels allows guests to graze for the afternoon. Baby raspberry and coconut cakes, and little chocolate mud cakes can be prepared the day before and stored in airtight containers. Make the apple and honey tea cakes a few hours before serving. For a savoury touch, serve the ricotta, spinach and parmesan tarts, which can be made a day in advance and stored in the fridge until required.

LIQUID SUGGESTIONS

Serve a well-chilled fruit tea such as the nectarine and basil iced tea as well as a selection of other teas and herbal teas. It is easier for each guest to have their own tea infuser, so they can choose their tea, and serve flasks of hot water. If you are serving iced fruit teas or hot herbal fruit teas, sparkling white wine can be a good accompaniment.

tea for 2

banana and palm sugar wontons
winter liquorice tea

FOOD PREP

A cosy tea for 2 on a cold afternoon would be great with warm banana and palm sugar wontons and winter liquorice tea. Prepare and cook the wontons just before serving to ensure they are crisp.

LIQUID SUGGESTIONS

Share a pot of tea or serve the winter liquorice tea with shots of ouzo or pastis for extra warmth.

shower tea for 20

tea-soaked little pears
candied lemon and lime tarts
little chocolate mud cakes
ricotta, spinach and parmesan tarts

FOOD PREP

Set up a large table where people can serve themselves. A large bowl full of tea-soaked little pears (double the recipe), and plates of candied lemon and lime tarts (double the recipe), little chocolate mud cakes (double the recipe) and ricotta, spinach and parmesan tarts (double the recipe) will fill the table nicely. All of these recipes can be made a day in advance and stored in airtight containers in the fridge.

LIQUID SUGGESTIONS

Serve one or two different iced teas and a selection of hot teas as well as sparkling white wine and a fresh, slightly fruity riesling or an aged semillon.

afternoon tea for 6

tea-soaked little pears or baby raspberry and coconut cakes
green apple and vanilla tea sorbet or apple and honey tea cakes
wild raspberry and lime iced tea

FOOD PREP

On a warm summer day, you could serve the tea-soaked little pears with the green apple and vanilla tea sorbet, which can both be made a day in advance. On a cooler day, try the warm baby raspberry and coconut cakes or warm apple and honey tea cakes.

LIQUID SUGGESTIONS

On a warm day, serve the wild raspberry and lime iced tea (be sure to use good-quality wild raspberry tea). On a cooler day, serve hot teas such as lemon and ginger or a lightly smoked black tea.

glossary

arborio rice
Taking its name from a village in the Piedmont region of northern Italy, this short-grain rice is used for risotto. It releases some of its starch when cooked, making a creamy savoury rice dish. Other varieties used for risotto include violone and carnaroli. All are sometimes simply labelled "risotto rice".

beef stock

1½ kg (3 lb) beef bones, cut into pieces
2 onions, quartered
2 carrots, quartered
2 stalks celery, cut into large pieces
assorted fresh herbs
2 bay leaves
10 peppercorns
4 litres (16 cups or 128 fl oz) water

Preheat the oven to 220°C (425°F). Place the bones in a baking dish and bake for 30 minutes. Add the onions and carrots and bake for 20 minutes. Remove the bones, onions and carrots and place in a stockpot or large saucepan. Skim the fat from the top of the juices in the dish, then add 2 cups (16 fl oz) boiling water to remove all the juices from the dish. Pour the juices into the saucepan. Add the celery, herbs, bay leaves, peppercorns and water to the saucepan and bring to the boil. Allow the mixture to simmer for 4–5 hours or until the stock has a good flavour. Skim the top of the stock during the cooking time. Strain the stock and use as the recipe requires. Refrigerate the stock for up to 3 days or freeze for up to 3 months. Makes 2½–3 litres (10–12 cups or 80–96 fl oz).

betel leaves
Often called wild betel leaves or *cha plu*. The leaves are sold in bunches still on their stems. Remove the leaves from the stems and soak in cold water to refresh before using as wrappers for morsels of food or shredded in salads. Available from Asian food stores.

black sesame seeds
From the same family as white sesame seeds, only black. Substitute white sesame seeds. Available from Asian food stores.

bonito flakes
Fine shavings from a dried bonito fish fillet. They look like rose-coloured wood shavings and are used for making dashi,* a stock used extensively in Japanese cooking. Available from Japanese or Asian supermarkets.

brûlée iron
A thick, heavy disk of steel on a long handle. It is heated over gas or electric heat until very hot and then, in a sweeping motion, placed over the sugar on top of a crème brûlée to form a caramelised crust of sugar. "The brûlée iron caramelises the sugar very quickly so the crème does not melt. Avaliable from cooks' shops. If you cannot find a brûlée iron, a small blowtorch from the hardware store will do the trick.

caper berries
The flower of the caper bush becomes an oval berry or fruit, which is full of tiny seeds. Caper berries are sold with tender stems attached in vinegar or a brine solution. Available from good delicatessens.

chervil
A delicate, lacey-looking herb with a faint, sweet aniseed flavour. Its flavour diminishes after being chopped, so add to food just before serving.

chicken stock

1½ kg (3 lb) chicken bones, cut into pieces
2 onions, quartered
2 carrots, quartered
2 stalks celery, cut into large pieces
assorted fresh herbs
2 bay leaves
10 peppercorns
4 litres (16 cups or 128 fl oz) water

Place all of the ingredients in a stockpot or large saucepan and simmer for 3–4 hours or until the stock is well flavoured. Skim the fat from the top of the stock during the cooking time. Strain and use as the recipe requires. Refrigerate for up to 3 days or freeze for up to 3 months. Makes 2½–3 litres (10–12 cups or 80–96 fl oz).

chilli oil
Oil infused with the heat and flavour of chillies. Different brands have different strengths. Available from Asian food stores and some supermarkets.

Chinese barbecue duck
A cooked duck, spiced and barbecued in the traditional Chinese style. Available from Chinese barbecue shops or from Chinese food stores.

Chinese barbecue pork
Cooked pork meat, spiced and barbecued in the traditional Chinese barbecue style. Also known as char sui. Available from Chinese barbecue shops or from Chinese food stores.

corella pears
Also known as cocktail pears, these small sweet pears are great for eating or poaching.

dariole moulds
Small cylindrical metal moulds with slightly sloping sides used to make puddings or set mousse in.

dashi broth

4 cups (32 fl oz) cold water
5cm (2 in) piece kombu (dried giant seaweed)
3 tablespoons dried bonito flakes*

Place the water and kombu in a saucepan and heat until almost boiling. Before the water boils, remove the kombu. (If the water boils with the kombu in it, the dashi will have a bad odour.) The kombu should be soft when removed, which indicates enough flavour has been released. Place the bonito flakes in the saucepan and bring to the boil. As soon as the water boils, remove the pan from the heat and allow to stand for 5 minutes before straining. The dashi is now ready to use as the recipe requires.

demerara sugar
A dark sugar with hard, dry crystals. The colour comes from molasses. Substitute dark brown sugar if necessary.

fish stock

1 tablespoon butter
1 onion, finely chopped
750g (1½ lb) fish bones, chopped
1 cup (8 fl oz) white wine
1 litre (32 fl oz) water
10 peppercorns
3–4 sprigs mild herbs
1 bay leaf

Place the butter and onion in a large saucepan over low heat and cook for 10 minutes or until the onion is soft but not browned. Add the fish bones, wine, water, peppercorns, herbs and bay leaf and simmer for 20 minutes. Skim the top of the stock at intervals. Strain and allow to cool. Use the stock as the recipe requires. Refrigerate the stock for up to 2 days or freeze for 2 months. Makes 3–3½ cups (750–875ml or 24–28 fl oz).
Note: do not simmer the stock for more than 20 minutes or it will sour.

framboise
Raspberry-flavoured brandy.

galangal
Looks similar to ginger but with a pink tinge, and can be purchased fresh or sliced and bottled in brine.

glutinous rice
Predominantly used in sweets, glutinous rice is made up of plump, opaque grains of either white, black, short- or long-grain rice. The grains become sticky and sweet when cooked. Soak glutinous rice overnight before using if you are steaming it, or use it unsoaked if you are cooking it by the absorption method. Available from Asian supermarkets.

green tea soba noodles
A speciality from northern Japan, these fine noodles are made from wheat flour and flavoured with green tea. Available from Japanese and Asian supermarkets.

haloumi
Firm, salty white cheese made from sheep's milk. It has a stringy texture and is usually sold in brine. Available from delicatessens and some supermarkets.

hoisin sauce
A thick, sweet-tasting Chinese sauce made from fermented soy beans, sugar, salt and red rice. Use it as a dipping or glazing sauce. Available from Asian food stores and supermarkets.

kaffir lime
The fragrant leaves are crushed or shredded and used in cooking, and the limes are used for their juice and rind mainly in Thai cuisine. Both the limes (fresh) and the leaves (available in packets, fresh or dried) are available from Asian grocers.

lemongrass
A tall lemon-scented grass used in Asian, mainly Thai, cooking. Peel away the outer leaves and use the tender root-end of the grass.

mascarpone
An Italian triple-cream curd-style fresh cheese, which has a similar consistency to double or thick cream. Available from delicatessens and some supermarkets.

miso
A thick paste made from fermented and processed soy beans. Red miso is a combination of barley and soy beans and yellow miso is a combination of rice and soy beans.

non-reactive bowl
A ceramic or glass bowl, often necessary when high concentrations of vinegar or acid foods are used.

non-reactive saucepan
Often necessary when high concentrations of vinegar or acid foods are used. Use any saucepan except a saucepan made from aluminium (such as stainless steel or heatproof glass).

nori

Thin sheets of dried and often toasted seaweed. Nori is used to wrap sushi and it is also added to Japanese soups. If you purchase untoasted nori, toast nori sheets over a low flame for 3 seconds on each side before using. Available in packets of sheets from Asian supermarkets.

proving

Process when a yeast mixture or dough is left covered in a warm, draught-free place to rise or prove.

ramekins

Small, ovenproof dishes used for soufflés, crème brûlées and other individually served foods.

rice paper

The white rectangular paper often found on the outside of nougat and sweets. Available from delicatessens and speciality food stores.

rice paper rounds

Fine, transparent circles made from a paste of rice and water. Before using, brush or dip in water until pliable. Available from Asian supermarkets.

roma tomatoes

Also known as egg tomatoes, these oval shaped tomatoes are great for cooking and eating.

shiitake mushrooms

Originally from Japan and Korea, these mushrooms have a distinctive woody and almost meaty flavour. They have brownish tops with a creamy underside. Available from fruit and vegetable stores.

shortcrust pastry

2 cups plain (all-purpose) flour
155g (5 oz) butter, chopped
iced water

Place the flour and butter in a food processor and process until mixture has formed fine crumbs. Add enough iced water to form a soft dough. Remove dough from food processor and knead lightly. Wrap the dough in plastic wrap and refrigerate for 30 minutes before rolling to prevent shrinkage when baked. Makes 1 quantity.

sterilised jar

Before putting foods into jars to be sealed and stored, the jars need to be sterilised. Sterilise jars by thoroughly washing in hot water. Place them on a baking tray, place in a preheated 100°C (200°F) oven and allow to heat for 30 minutes. Remove, fill and seal.

sushi rice

1½ cups short-grain rice
2 cups (16 fl oz) water
5cm (2 in) piece kombu (dried giant seaweed)
⅓ cup (2¾ fl oz) rice vinegar
2 teaspoons sugar
salt

Place the rice in a colander and wash well under running water. Place in a saucepan with the water and place the kombu on top of the rice. Cover and cook over medium heat. Remove the kombu when the water boils. Continue cooking, covered, and boiling for 2 minutes. Reduce the heat to low and cook, covered, for 15 minutes or until all the liquid has been absorbed. Place the rice in a glass or ceramic bowl and toss with a wooden spoon or paddle until warm. Combine the vinegar, sugar and salt. While tossing the rice, sprinkle over the vinegar mixture. Continue tossing the rice until it is cool. Cover with a damp cloth until ready to use. Makes 1 quantity.
Note: when cooking rice, be sure to use a tight-fitting lid on the saucepan.

sweet flaky pastry

2 cups plain (all-purpose) flour
2 tablespoons caster (superfine) sugar
60g (2 oz) butter
150ml (5 fl oz) water
125g (4 oz) butter, extra, chopped

Process the flour, sugar and butter in a food processor until the mixture has formed fine crumbs. While the motor is running, add the water and process to form a smooth dough.
Roll out the dough on a lightly floured surface until 45cm (18 in) long and 2cm (¾ in) thick.
Soften the extra butter until pliable but not melted. Spread over two-thirds of the pastry. Take the pastry with no butter and fold it over one-third of the pastry. Fold the pastry over again to encase the butter. Press the edges to seal. Cover and refrigerate for 15 minutes before rolling to use. Makes 1 quantity.

sweet shortcrust pastry

2 cups plain (all-purpose) flour
3 tablespoons caster (superfine) sugar
155g (5 oz) butter, chopped
iced water

Process the flour, sugar and butter in a food processor to form fine crumbs. Add enough iced water to form a soft dough. Remove the

dough from the food processor and knead lightly.
Wrap in plastic wrap and refrigerate for 30 minutes. Makes 1 quantity.

Szechwan peppercorns

Not really peppercorns at all, these are small, red-brown dried berries, native to the Chinese province of Szechwan. They have a very distinctive fragrance and flavour. Roast or heat them before crushing. Avaliable from Asian supermarkets.

tahini

A thick, smooth paste made from lightly toasted and ground sesame seeds. Available in jars from supermarkets.

udon noodles

White Japanese wheat noodles, which can be purchased fresh (in the refrigerator section) or dried. They come in a variety of thicknesses and lengths. Available from Japanese or Asian supermarkets.

vanilla beans

The fermented and dried seed pods of an orchid native to Mexico. They are long and dark, and good-quality beans are flexible and fragrant. Available from quality food stores and some supermarkets. Substitute 1 teaspoon quality vanilla extract if unavailable.

vegetable stock

4 litres (16 cups or 128 fl oz) water
1 parsnip
2 onions, quartered
1 clove garlic, peeled
2 carrots, quartered
300g (10 oz) roughly chopped cabbage
3 stalks celery, cut into large pieces

small bunch mixed fresh herbs
2 bay leaves
1 tablespoon peppercorns

Place all the ingredients in a saucepan or stockpot and allow to simmer for 2 hours or until the stock has a good flavour. Skim the top of the stock at intervals. Strain the stock and use as the recipe requires. Refrigerate the stock for up to 4 days or freeze for up to 8 months. Makes 2½–3 litres (10–12 cups or 80–96 fl oz).

wasabi

A knobbly green root of the Japanese plant *Wasabia japonica*. Wasabi has the same warming or stinging nasal sensation as horseradish, and is used with sushi and sashimi. Available in paste or powdered form from Asian grocers.

wonton wrappers

Thin squares or rounds of dough used to enclose fillings when making dumplings in Chinese cuisine. Available fresh or frozen from Asian food stores.

cup conversions

1 cup almonds, whole = 155g (5 oz)
1 cup baby English spinach leaves = 60g (2 oz)
1 cup basil leaves, whole, firmly packed = 50g (1¾ oz)
1 cup berries, mixed, chopped = 220g (7 oz)
1 cup cheese, parmesan, finely grated = 100g (3¼ oz)
1 cup coconut cream = 250g (8 oz)
1 cup coconut, desiccated = 90g (3 oz)
1 cup coriander (cilantro) leaves, whole = 30g (1 oz)
1 cup couscous = 185g (6 oz)
1 cup flour, plain (all-purpose) and self-raising (self-rising) = 125g (4 oz)
1 cup flour, wholemeal = 150g (5 oz)
1 cup honey = 350g (11¼ oz)
1 cup olives, medium green, unpitted = 175g (5¾ oz)
1 cup parsley, flat-leaf, whole = 20g (¾ oz)
1 cup polenta = 150g (5 oz)
1 cup raspberries, whole = 125g (4 oz)
1 cup rice, arborio, uncooked = 220g (7 oz)
1 cup rocket (arugula) leaves, roughly chopped = 45g (1½ oz)
1 cup sour cream = 250g (8 oz)
1 cup sugar, caster (superfine) = 250g (8 oz)
1 cup sugar, demerara = 220g (7 oz)
1 cup yoghurt, plain = 250g (8 oz)

index

Index compiled by Russell Brooks